BLUEGRASS WITH Friends

Group-Friendly Bluegrass Instruction Series

Guitar
BOOK 1

Cover design by Marla Goodman
Cover photos by Tyson Vick
Editorial development by Shawna Lockhart

© 2018 Parsons Studios
Bozeman, MT 59715

All rights reserved. This book may not be reproduced
in any form without written permission from the publisher.

1 2 ③ 4 5 6 7 8 9 10

bluegrasswithfriends.com

This book is dedicated to my wife, Linda.

About Bluegrass with Friends

Playing music with friends, family, or even with a group of brand new acquaintances is one of the joys of life. People of all ages can come together playing and singing traditional songs. **Bluegrass with Friends** is a uniquely group-friendly series in that it teaches a matching set of 12 songs in coordinating books for guitar, banjo, mandolin, fiddle and bass. Now it's easy to start a jam group with friends. Using this book, you will gain valuable skills while learning songs that you can play right away by yourself or in a group setting. You can also watch and listen to Mike demonstrating songs in accompanying online videos.

In addition to skills and techniques for your instrument and helpful tips and tricks, this series focuses on how to play as part of a group. You will learn how (and when) to play backup, so that when another player is soloing or singing the melody, you can contribute to the music without overwhelming it. And of course, you will learn to play interesting, tasteful leads for when it's your turn to shine.

About Mike Parsons

When Mike was nine, he, his father, and his grandfather began playing fiddle. His family joined the Idaho Old Time Fiddlers Organization and soon he was playing around Idaho with the Junior Jammers. The Parsons Family Band formed and ten-year old Mike, his mother, sisters, and brothers played barn dances, gyms, and shows across Idaho. Mike won the Junior Idaho State Fiddle Championship in 1973 and the Golden Spike Fiddle Championship that same year.

Since then, Mike has continued to play professionally with a variety of bands and added mandolin, guitar, banjo, bass, dobro, and steel guitar to instruments he plays. Most of all, Mike has been a patient and passionate teacher of music for more than 40 years. His enthusiasm for sharing bluegrass music shows throughout the **Bluegrass with Friends** series.

The Parsons Family: (L-R) Don (Dad/fiddle), Mike (fiddle), LaDene (Mom/piano), Kathy (mando), twins DeeAnn (banjo) and JoAnn (guitar), Jeff "Pig" (fiddle), Billy (bass). Donny (not pictured, drums).

On the Cover: Mike's guitar was made by Kevin Kopp in Bozeman, Montana.

Contents

Welcome to the Guitar 1
Playing the Guitar 2
What You Will Need to Get Started 2
Learning the Guitar Neck 4
Single-string G Scale 5
Chords 6
Reading Tablature 7
Counting in Music 7
Getting Ready to Play a Song 7
Chords for the Key of G 8
Practice Strumming 8
Practice Changing Chords 8
Strumming Chords 8
Alternating Bass Note/Strum 9
Long Journey Home Rhythm Tab 9
Long Journey Home Melody Guitar Tab ... 10
Long Journey Home Lyrics/Chord Chart ... 11
The 1st Position G Scale 12
Little Birdie Melody Guitar Tab 13
Mama Don't 'Low Mixed Bass/Strum Rhythm ... 14
Mama Don't 'Low Melody Guitar Tab 15
Using a Capo to Change the Key 16
Tips for Using a Capo 16
Playing a Slide 18
Will the Circle Be Unbroken
    Melody Guitar Tab 19
Will the Circle Be Unbroken Rhythm 20
Will the Circle Be Unbroken Lyrics 21
Playing a Pull-Off 22
Harmonics 23
G Lick with Slide, Pull-off, and Harmonic ... 23
Giving the Count 24

Hand Me Down My Walking Cane
    Rhythm Guitar Tab 24
Hand Me Down My Walking Cane
    Melody Guitar Tab 25
Playing a Hammer-on 26
Nobody's Business Melody Guitar Tab ... 27
Chord Numbering 28
Playing an Intro/Turnaround/Ending Lick ... 28
Late Last Night Melody Guitar Tab 29
John Henry Rhythm Guitar Tab 30
John Henry Melody Guitar Tab 31
Movable F-Shape Chord 32
Little Maggie Rhythm Guitar Tab 32
Little Maggie Melody Guitar Tab 33
Playing in 3/4 Time 34
Down in the Willow Garden Rhythm 34
Down in the Willow Garden
    Melody Guitar Tab 36
Playing Minor Chords 38
Relative Minor Scale 38
Minor Chord Recipe 38
Shady Grove Melody Guitar Tab 39
Shady Grove Rhythm 39
Chords for the Key of D 40
D Scale 40
Movable D Scale 40
Angeline the Baker Melody Guitar Tab ... 41
Guitar Picking Practice 42
Basic Guitar Chords 43
Getting Started with Guitar Chord Shapes ... 44
Closed Chord Groups 45

Welcome to the Guitar

You're in luck! You have chosen to learn the guitar. Whether it is because you always wanted to play Layla like Eric Clapton, or you just want to have lots of good, clean fun, you have embarked on a course of learning you won't regret. This page shows the basic parts of the guitar.

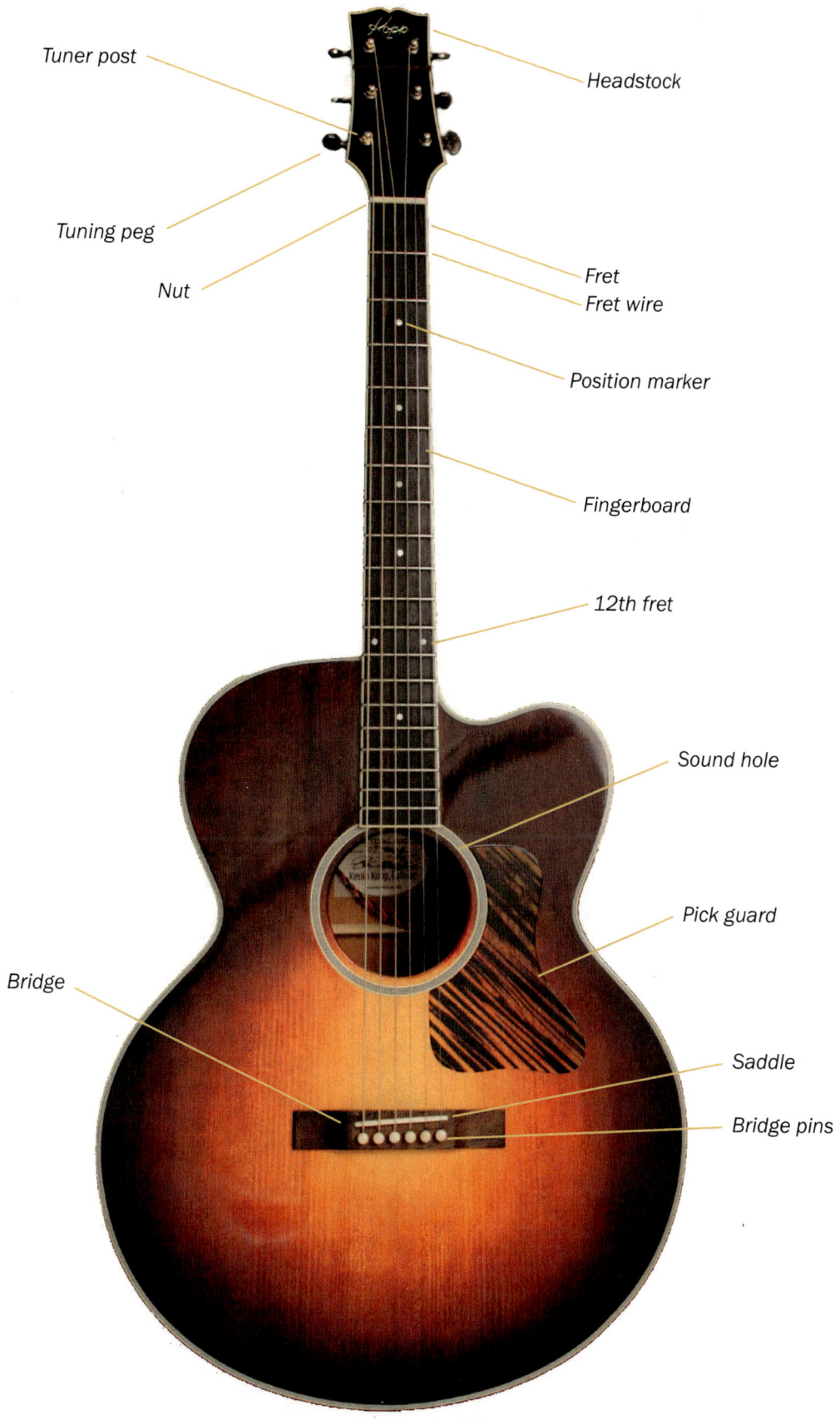

Playing the Guitar

This book introduces you to playing the guitar by learning specific skills and then right away applying those skills to songs you can play with friends or on your own. Use the on-line videos that accompany the book for more playing tips. You can find links to the videos at bluegrasswithfriends.com. Other books in this series teach the same songs on other instruments such as banjo, mandolin, fiddle, ukulele and bass to make it easy for you to start jamming with your friends. You can find these books at bluegrasswithfriends.com.

What You Will Need to Get Started

Picks

For bluegrass guitar, you will need a flat pick. Flat picks are usually hard plastic but you can find tortoise shell, carbon fiber, and other special materials. A plastic pick is just fine. Get used to the feel of using a flat pick by starting to use it right away.

Grip the pick between your thumb and index finger. Bend the tip of your thumb to grip the pick. This helps keep your wrist and fingers flexible.

Hold the pick perpendicular to the strings.

You can experiment with changing your pick angle to produce a brighter or more melow tone.

Strap

A guitar strap helps you support the guitar, especially when standing, which is common when playing bluegrass music. When you are practicing, try standing as well as sitting. The strap should hold the guitar comfortably. Attach the strap via the button where the neck joins the body and to the guitar's end pin (where the electronics jack may also be located). This gives you a better position than tying the strap to the headstock of the guitar. If you don't have a button where the neck meets the body, have one installed by your music store or a professional luthier. When holding the guitar, don't press the guitar tightly against your chest as that may dampen the tone.

Tuner

Tune your guitar frequently. Unless you already have perfect pitch, you should purchase an electronic tuner. You can get one that will work great for about $20. Even when you are practicing by yourself, play in tune so you are used to hearing standard pitches.

Guitar

Oh, yeah, you will also need a guitar that suits you. Buy the best one you can afford. A $1000 guitar only costs $3 a day over the course of a year, but you can probably find a quite nice one for under $500.

Keep your tuner handy and tune your guitar frequently

Hold the guitar so that the sound hole is in line with the center of your chest. Adjust your strap so that the guitar is in a comfortable position. Hold the guitar slightly out from your torso, so that you don't dampen its tone.

Learning the Guitar Neck

The first step is to learn the notes and where they are on the guitar neck. Half steps are basic increments in the musical scale. When you look at the guitar neck, each fret is a half-step scale tone. Place your finger near, but slightly behind, the fret. Try each string as you go along, moving up in half tones. Guess what? 2 half tones make 1 whole step.

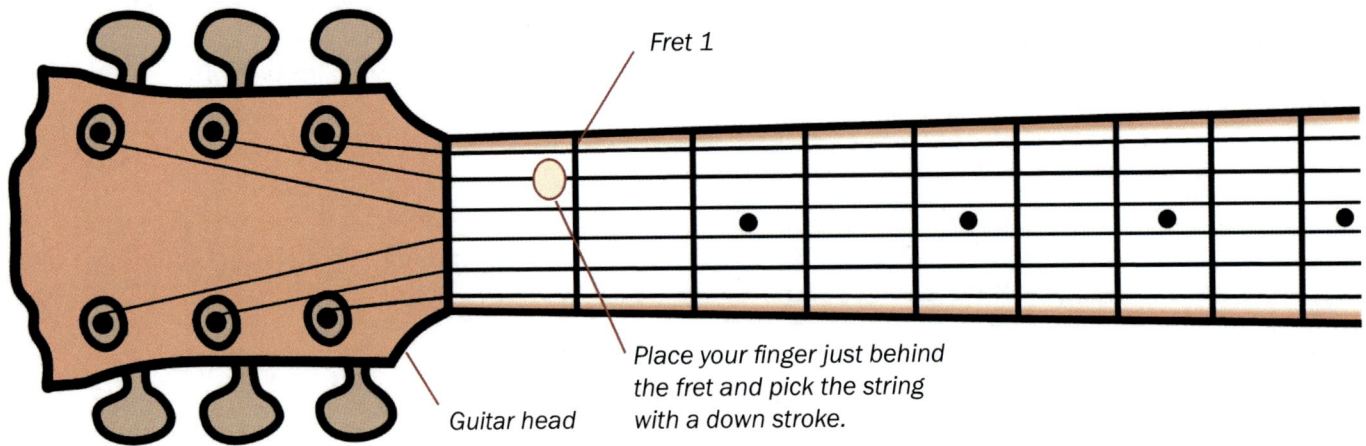

Notes in Standard Tuning

Here are some of the notes on the guitar neck. Notice the ♯ (sharp) and ♭ (flat) symbols. These indicate notes that are a half-step up and a half-step down from the named note. As you can see the high and low pitched E-strings are the same note (but two octaves apart), so that makes it easy to remember them. Start by picking the open string and walk up the neck one fret at a time. Say the note names to yourself as you go. The pattern just keeps going up the neck.

BE Alert
Notice that there is no sharp/flat between the notes B and C and likewise between E and F. That is because those pairs of notes are only one half-step apart. Think of "BE Alert" to remind yourself of the notes (B & E) that are only a half tone from their higher neighbor note (C & F).

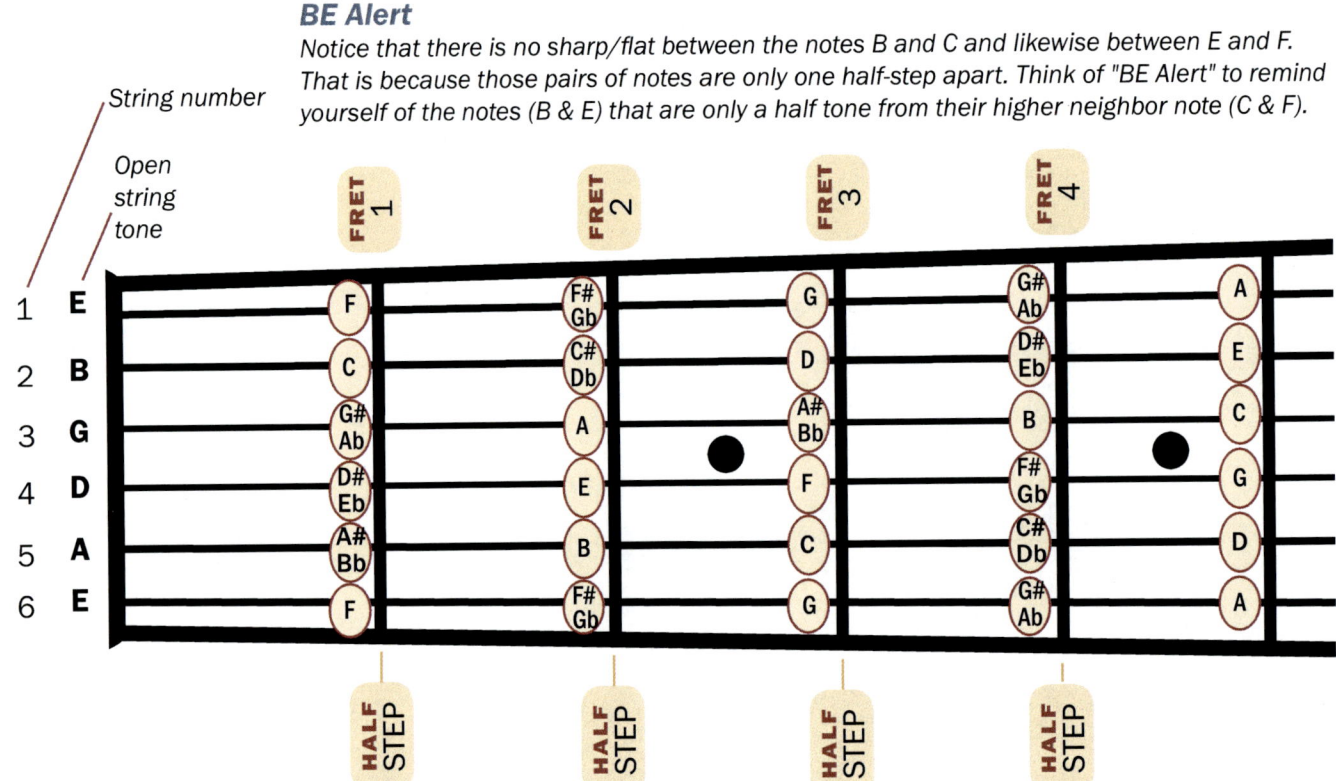

Major Scales

All of the major scales begin with a **root** tone (just fancy talk for the starting note), so the C major scale starts on C, the G major scale starts on G, and so forth. These are followed by tones in these intervals (or spacings):

WHOLE STEP, **WHOLE** STEP, **HALF** STEP, **WHOLE** STEP, **WHOLE** STEP, **WHOLE** STEP, **HALF** STEP

There are 8 tones in the scale and the last tone is the octave (double pitch frequency) of the starting tone. The only tricky part is that some of the note names have built-in steps. It sounds like they are evenly spaced, but they are *not*. For example, a C major scale goes like this:

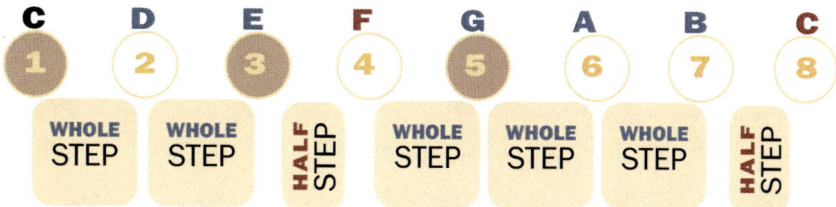

With the half-steps included, the scale has 12 tones. But we usually just play the 8 in the pattern mentioned above. Turns out that the note between a whole step has two names, one named for the note that is a half-step up from a note (like D♯) and the other (like E♭) that is a half-step down from the next higher note. Don't let that make your head hurt. Just accept it.

These half-steps are like the black keys on a piano

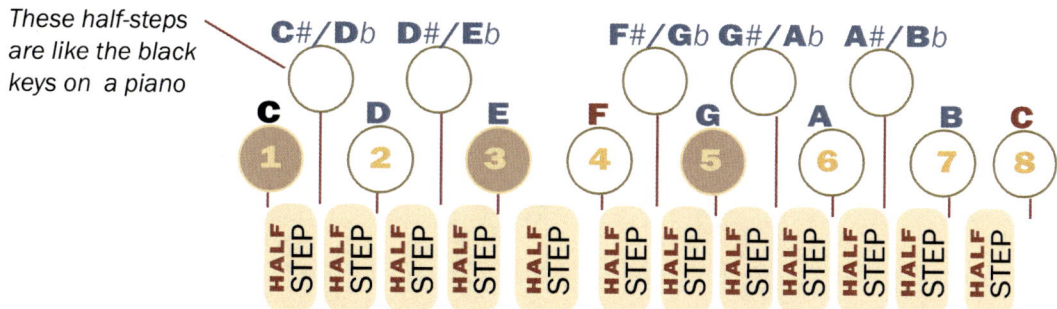

Single-string G Scale

Our first scale to learn for guitar is the G scale. Many bluegrass songs are played in the key of G, so it is a good starting point. This easy G scale just walks up the G string, using the major scale pattern:

	WHOLE STEP	WHOLE STEP	HALF STEP	WHOLE STEP	WHOLE STEP	WHOLE STEP	HALF STEP	
I		II	III	IV	V	VI	VII	I (VIII)
G		A	B	C	D	E	F#	G

Scale tones may also be referred to by numbers written as Roman numerals.

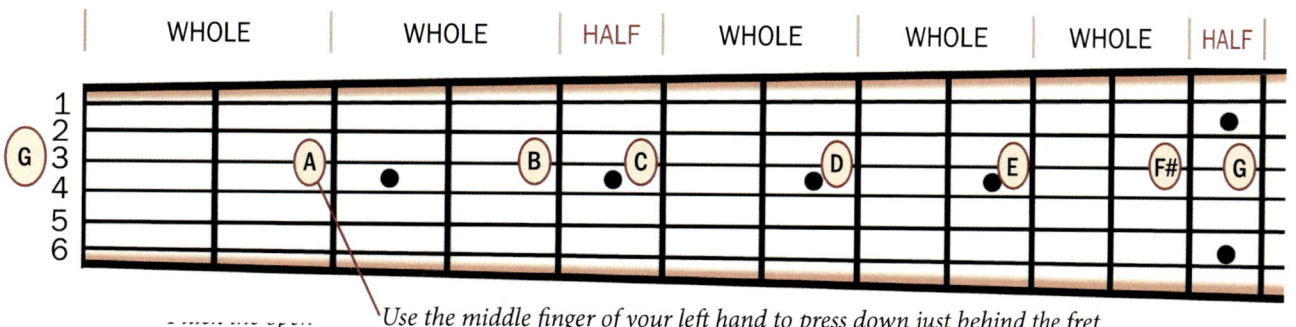

G string for the first note.

Use the middle finger of your left hand to press down just behind the fret.
Use the least amount of pressure you can apply to still get a clear tone.

Chords

Chords are made by using more than one tone together for a nice full sound. With just a few basic chords you can play many great bluegrass songs.

Chords are named by the types of tones included in them, like a recipe. The intervals (or musical spacing) between the notes in the chord make up the recipe. For now we are going to use *major chords*.

Major Chords

The C chord has these notes: C (the 1), E (the 3) and G (the 5) of the C scale. All of the major chords have this same 1, 3, 5 recipe, though the 1, 3, and 5 are not always in that order, and sometimes they are not all included either.

Different chords start from different root starting notes. Now that you know the "secret recipe" you can figure out other major chords; just use the 1st, 3rd, and 5th notes of their scale.

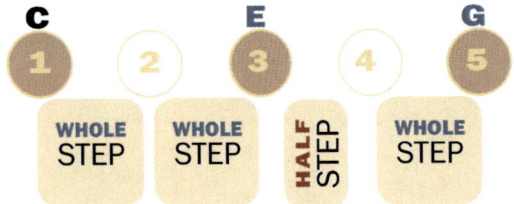

To make it easy to figure out where to put your fingers on the guitar neck, chords are usually pictured like this:

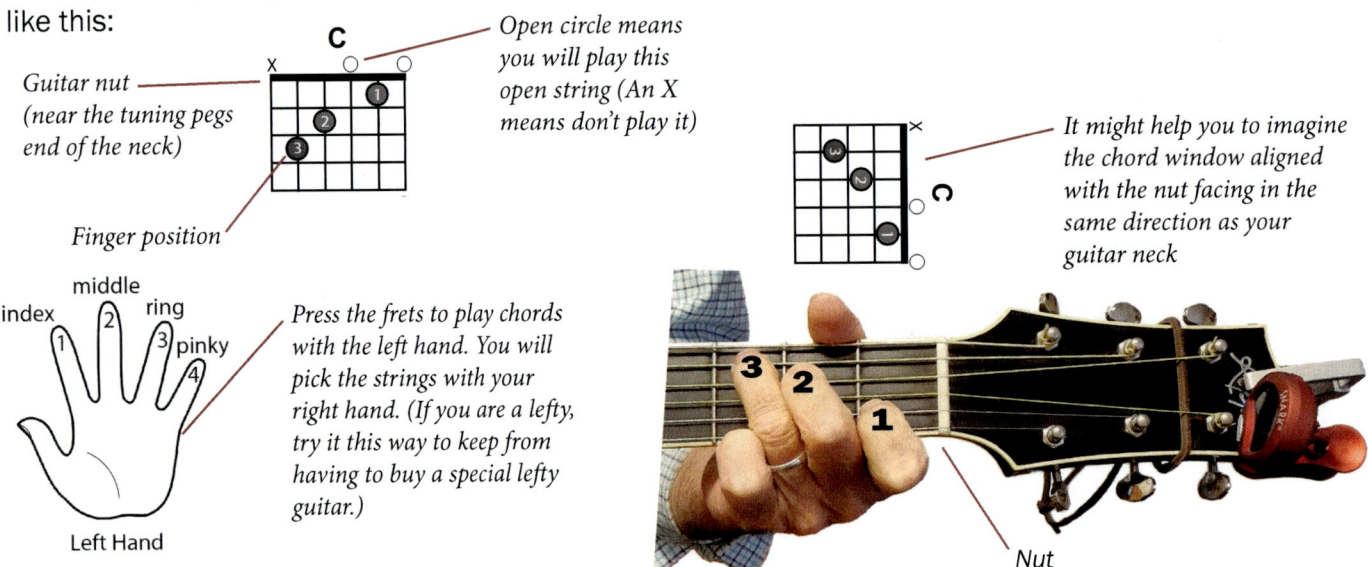

Guitar nut (near the tuning pegs end of the neck)

Open circle means you will play this open string (An X means don't play it)

Finger position

It might help you to imagine the chord window aligned with the nut facing in the same direction as your guitar neck

Press the frets to play chords with the left hand. You will pick the strings with your right hand. (If you are a lefty, try it this way to keep from having to buy a special lefty guitar.)

Left Hand

Nut

In this book, information about the chord is shown below the chord diagram. The note names are listed; for example, string 5 fret 3 is the note C, string 4 fret 2 is E, open string 3 is G, string 2 fret 1 is C, and open string 1 is E. The scale tone numbers are listed below the notes. For example, for the C chord we use the C major scale where is C is I, E is III (3) and G is V (5). Roman numerals are used for the scale tones. Learning which notes and scale tones make up the chord will help you play melodies by "ear". To start with, try to learn which string is used for the root tone (I) of the chord.

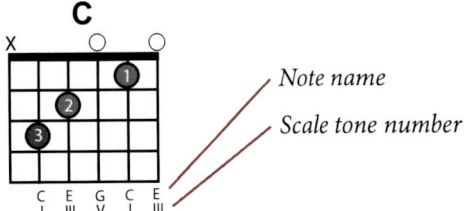

Note name

Scale tone number

Reading Tablature

The *tablature* (tab for short) for the first song is on the next page. The tab is like a picture of the guitar neck, but with numbers showing you which fret to press on which string. Each vertical line divides the musical *measures* in time. Many measures in guitar songs will have 8 notes per measure. These are called eighth notes. The first measure in the example shown below shows quarter notes; the second measure shows eighth notes.

The numbers in the tab show which fret to press down. If you have trouble picturing it, try laying your guitar parallel to the tab in the tab in the book. The tab is like a top view of the guitar neck over the time period of the song.

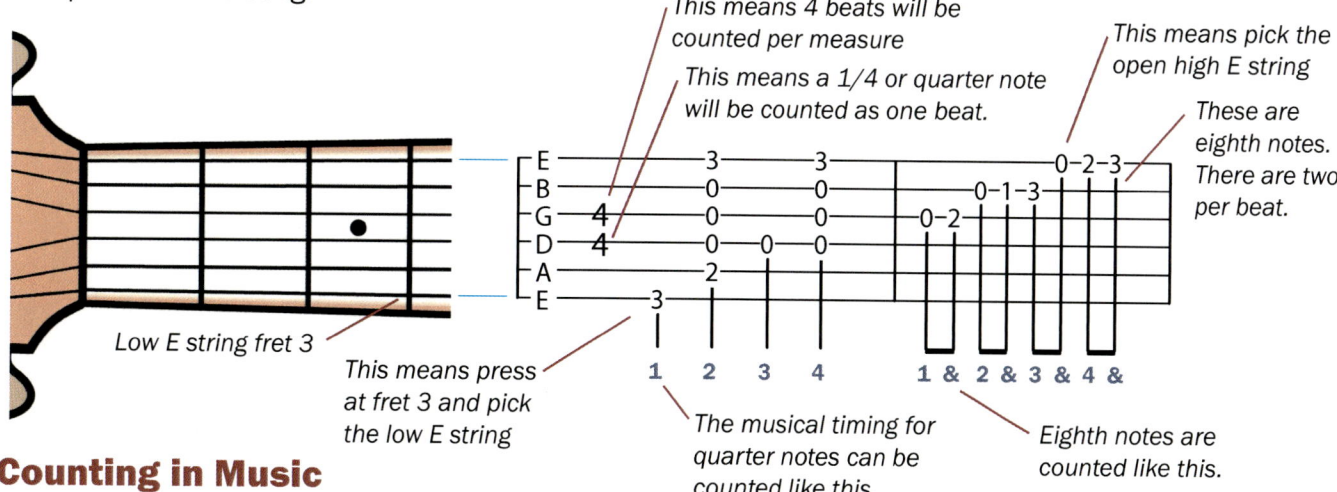

Counting in Music

The horizontal lines of the tab tell you which string and fret the note is on. The tail of the note tells you its counted value. Bluegrass music is often in 4/4 time. This means that there are 4 beats per measure and each quarter note gets one beat. You can count this 1 2 3 4. Bluegrass music often uses eight notes per measure. Two eighth notes fit in the same length of time as a single quarter note. They are counted 1 *and* 2 *and* 3 *and* 4 *and*...

Getting Ready to Play a Song

You can learn more about scales, chords, and music theory while you are playing some great traditional songs on the guitar. You will learn *Long Journey Home* in the key of G. Two components of playing a song are the rhythm and the melody. When you are singing a song, generally you are singing the melody. guitar solos, or solos on other instruments, are embellished versions of the melody. The rhythm part is provided by guitars strumming chords or mandolins and other instruments "chucking" the chords.

Practice the skills for each song. These skills build on each other and help you improve your guitar technique so that soon you will be able to hear a song and then play it on the guitar.

Playing Rhythm

Good rhythm playing is an important skill. When you are jamming with other people, you will play rhythm during the time they are playing the melody lead and vice versa. In fact, in bluegrass playing it is considered rude or just downright wrong-headed to play the melody over the top of the singer or another lead player. Of course there are exceptions to every rule, such as playing a tasteful harmony, but beginners generally need to work on good rhythm skills. If there are 4 players, your turn at playing lead will be at most 25% of the time. The other 75% of the time, you will be playing rhythm, or even not playing if there is so much sound that it overpowers the lead player or vocalist.

Providing a strong rhythmic backup really adds to the music. It creates the driving beat. Becoming proficient at playing chords and rhythm makes it easy for you to add to a jam or band setting. Be sure to practice rhythm as well as practicing playing the melodies. Use the play-along videos at the MT Music Lessons YouTube channel or at bluegrasswithfriends.com.

Chords for the Key of G

G (the I chord in the key of G), C (IV) and D (V) are easy to play using these chord shapes. Learn both the G and G#2 chord shapes. The finger grouping often makes it quicker to change from G#2 to C and to D.

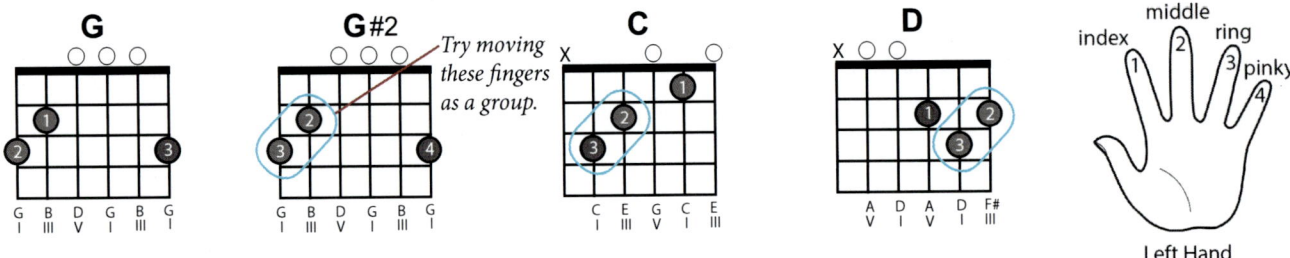

Practice Strumming

First practice strumming the open strings using just the right hand. Hold your pick with a firm grip and strum down toward the floor (v) on beat 1 and up (∧) on the "and" of the beat. Imagine you are the metronome. Move your strumming hand in time with the beat. Down, up, down, up – like clockwork.

Now practice just strumming the strings on the down beats (1, 2, 3, 4) and moving your hand upward in time (but don't hit the strings). Keep your same hand motion, just like clockwork, down, up, down, up.

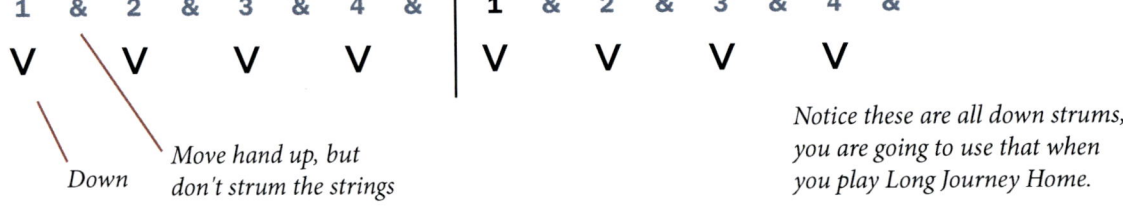

Practice Changing Chords

Now practice just the left hand. Move your left hand fingers from a G chord to a C chord shape. Do it 10 times without strumming, just move the left hand fingers. Then practice G to D ten times, C to D, D to G, C to G; you get the idea. You will start to develop coordination for your fingers. It just takes some practice.

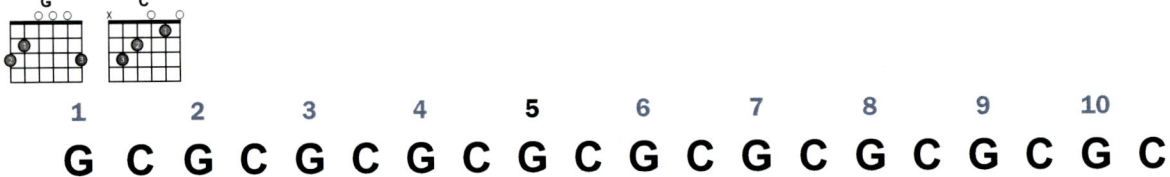

Don't strum, just use your left hand to make the silent chord shape.

Try the second fingering for G shown above. Can you move your 2nd and 3rd fingers to the C chord in a group?

Strumming Chords

Now put it all together and strum while changing chords. See Strumming Exercises on page 42 for more practice.

A slash means to strum the same chord as previously.

Alternating Bass Note/Strum

An often used rhythm in bluegrass guitar is to pick the root bass note (the I tone of the chord) then strum the chord, followed by picking the V (5) tone of the chord and another strum for a boom-chuck sound.

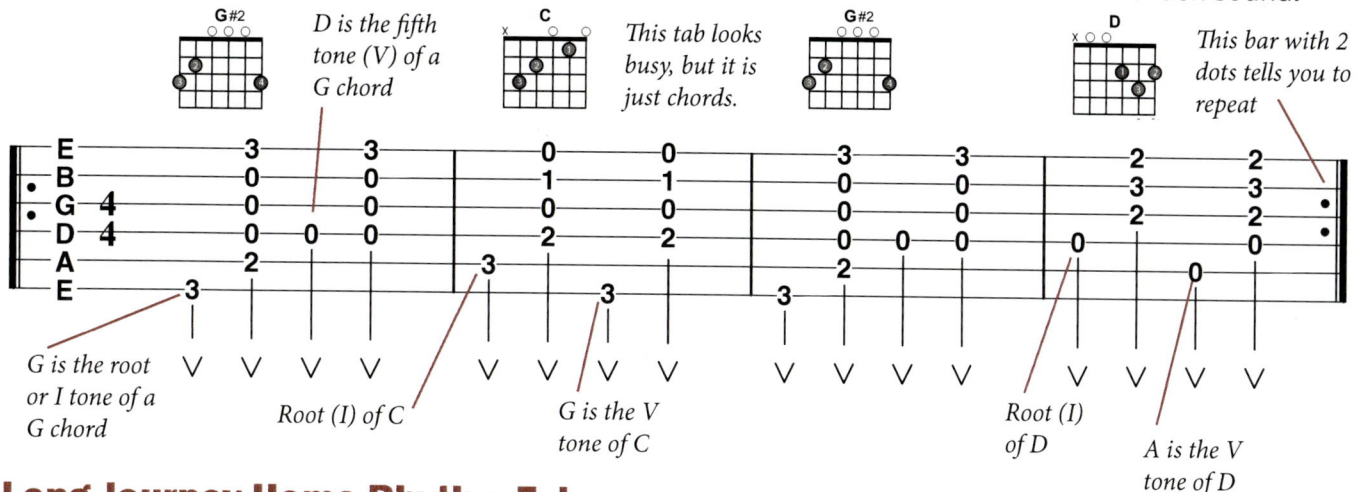

Long Journey Home Rhythm Tab

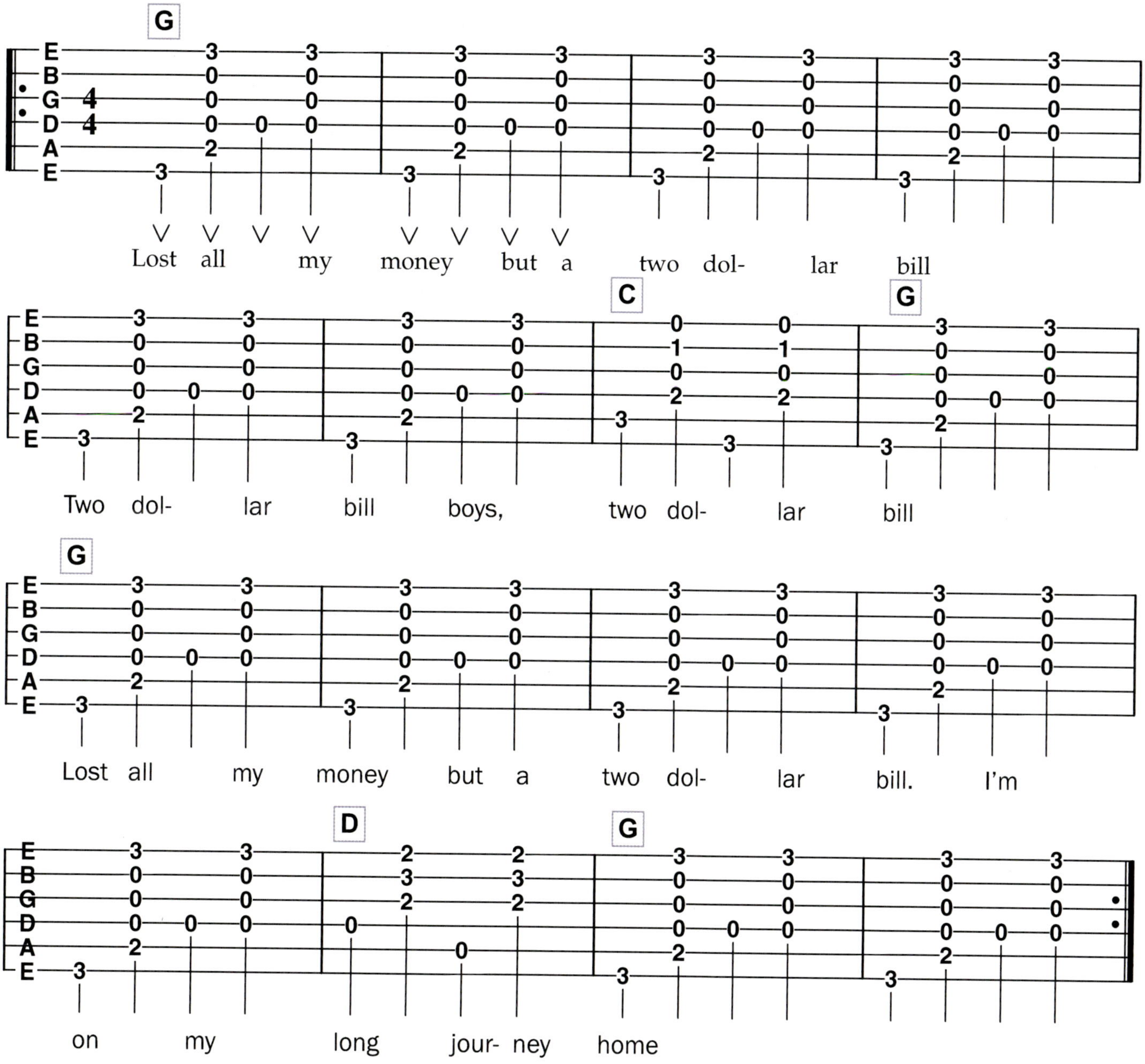

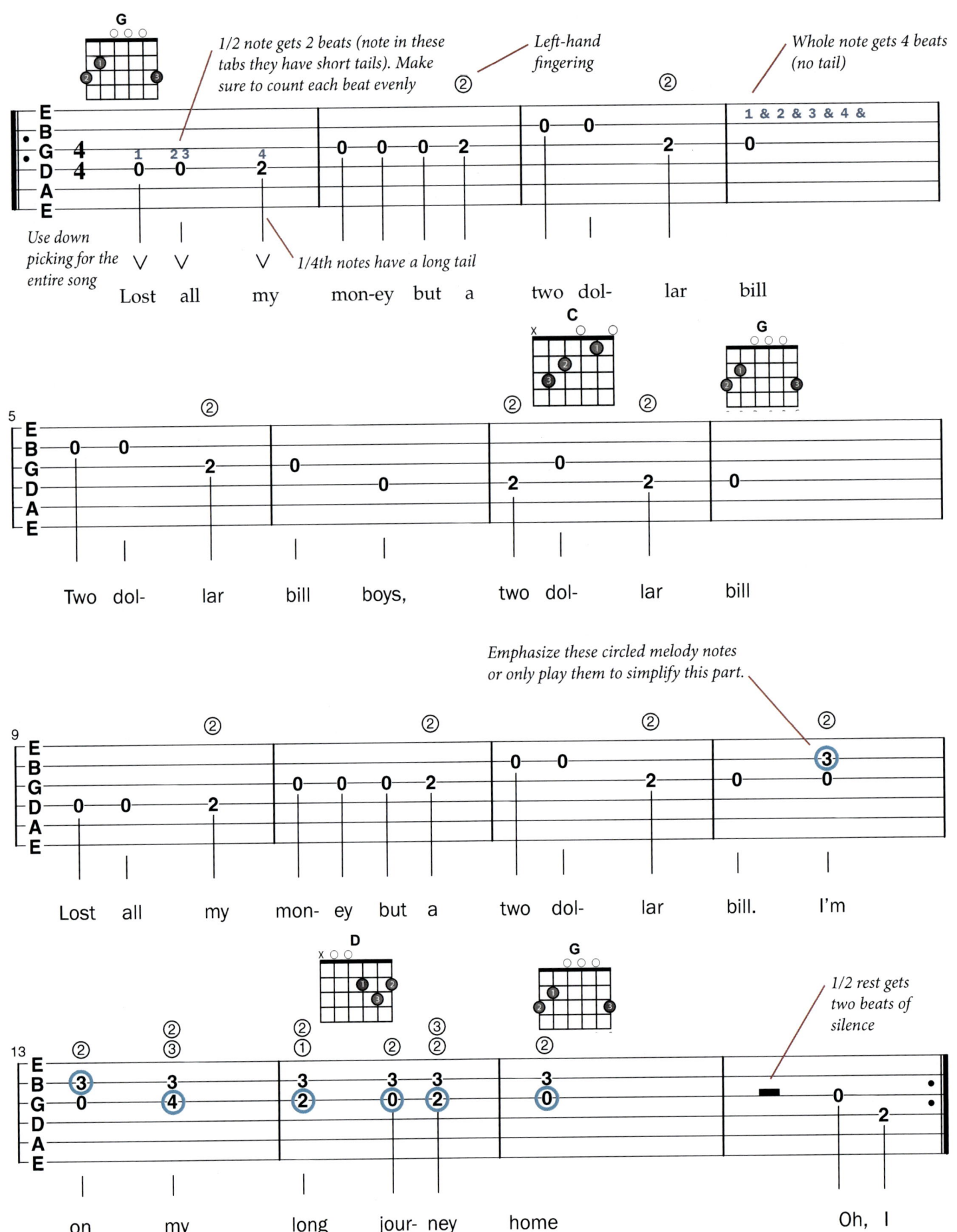

Long Journey Home Lyrics/Chord Chart

G (I)
Lost all my money but a two dollar bill
G (I)   C (IV)   G (I)
Two dollar bill boys, two dollar bill
G (I)
Lost all my money but a two dollar bill
G(I)   D (V)   G (I)
I'm on my long journey home

Cloudy in the west and it looks like rain
Looks like rain, boys, it looks like rain
Cloudy in the west and it looks like rain
I'm on my long journey home

It's dark and a-raining and I want to go home
Want to go home, boys, want to go home
Its dark and raining and I want to go home
I'm on my long journey home

Homesick and lonesome and I'm feeling kind of blue
Feeling kind of blue, boys, feeling kind of blue
Homesick and lonesome and I'm feeling kind of blue
I'm on my long journey home

There's black smoke a-rising and it surely is a train
Surely is a train boys, surely is a train
There's black smoke rising and it surely is a train
I'm on my long journey home

Tips for Efficient Practicing

- Review the Basic Guitar Chords on page 42. Practice the ones you are working on for a few minutes, quickly switching the left hand only for 10 times, then add the strum.
- Listen to a similar version of the song or watch the videos for this book. Become familiar with the melody. It is easier to learn to play the song if you can "hear" the melody in your head.
- When you are learning the song, start by playing the first measure (in bluegrass, usually a group of 4 or 8 notes). Sing or hum along. Think of the melody in your head. Try to bring out the melody clearly as you play it.
- Don't stop practicing the first time you get a section right. Play it right about 10 times so you store the correct version in your brain. Then move on to the next section.
- Quit practicing after a successful pass, so that the last thing in your brain is the correctly practiced version.
- Daily practice for 15 minutes will get better results than long practices done less frequently.
- Don't waste your time practicing a part you know. Warm up by practicing something familiar and then move on to a section you are having trouble with. Don't restart from the beginning of the song; work on a 4– or 8-note section until you get that right, then move on. When you can play each part, but it all together. Have fun playing!

Chords for Little Birdie in the Key of G

You should already be familiar with G and the D chords that you will use in Little Birdie.

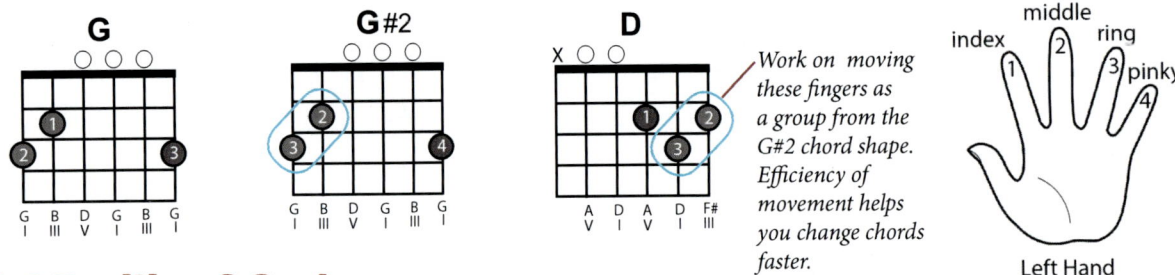

Work on moving these fingers as a group from the G#2 chord shape. Efficiency of movement helps you change chords faster.

The 1st Position G Scale

Remember the notes in the G scale: G A B C D E F# G.
Here is a version of the G scale to use for the song Little Birdie. Use the fingerings shown to reach the notes.

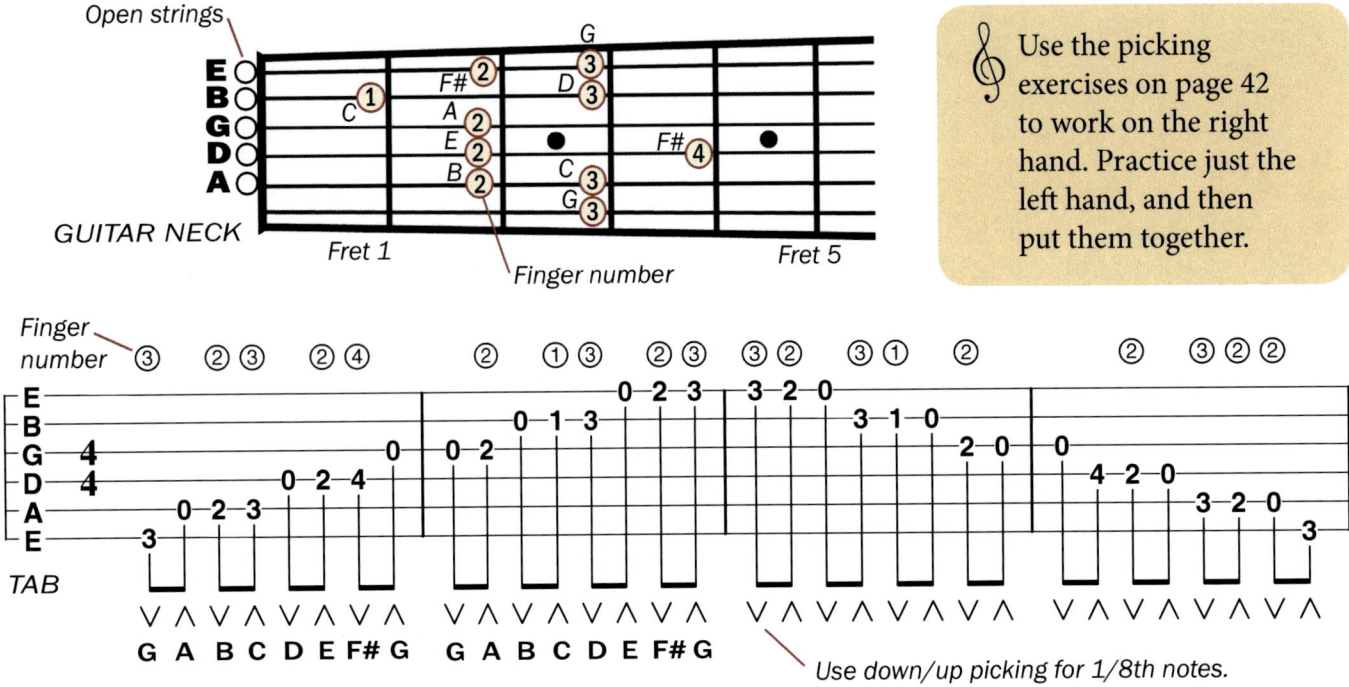

Use the picking exercises on page 42 to work on the right hand. Practice just the left hand, and then put them together.

Use down/up picking for 1/8th notes.

Little Birdie Rhythm Practice

For this song, use the bass note/strum rhythm like you used for Long Journey Home. Play the bass notes a bit louder and make your strum a quick "chuck". Listen to versions of this traditional song to learn to sing (or whistle) the melody. Play the rhythm using the chords shown on the melody tab.

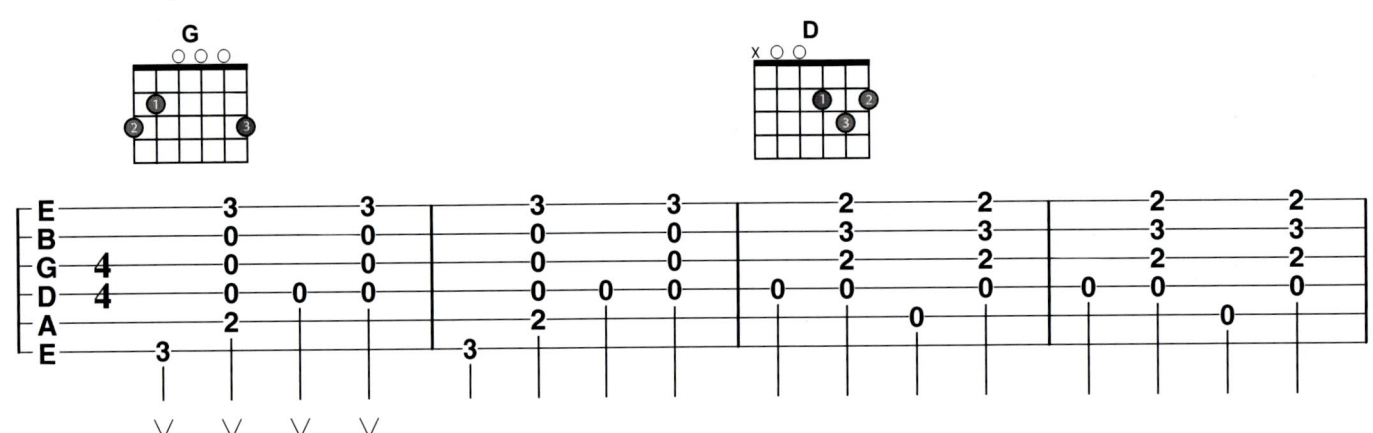

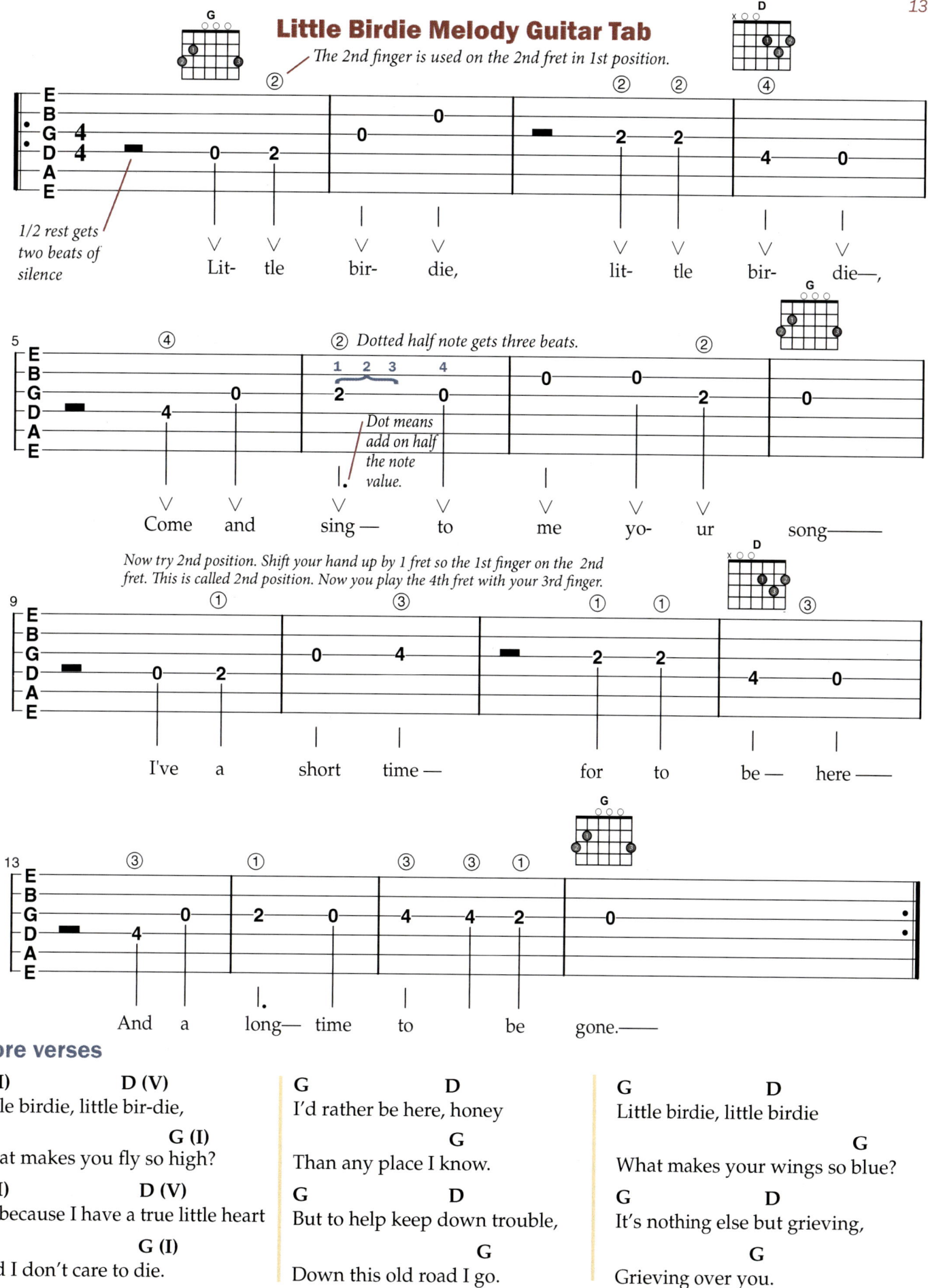

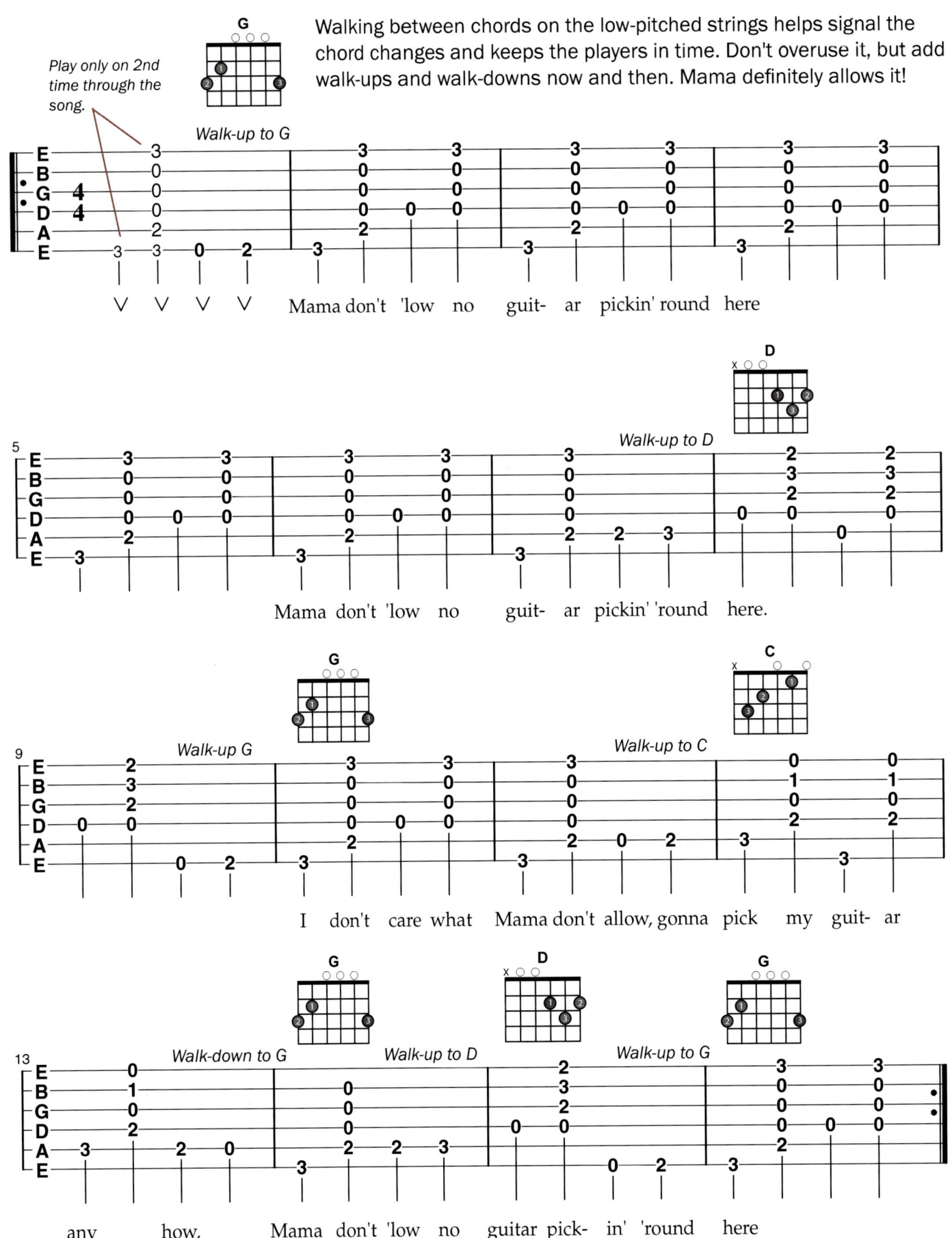

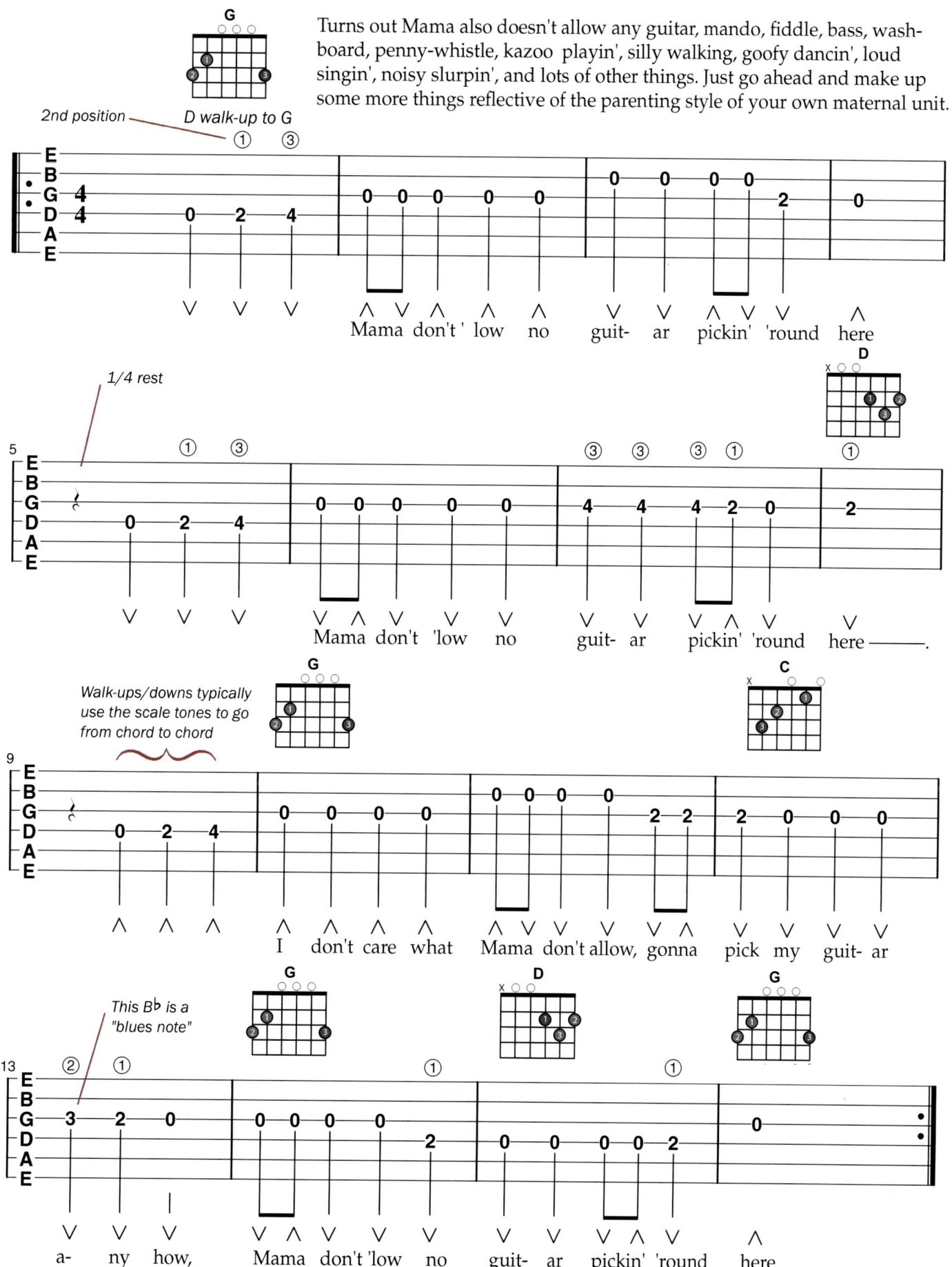

Using a Capo to Change the Key

You can use a capo to raise the pitch of your instrument. One of the most common reasons to do this is to select a *key* (a range of notes) convenient for singing. Singers may have a vocal range of only one octave (8 notes of the scale). The pitch of their voice determines the range of notes they can sing; for example, they may only be able to sing from note C to the next higher B note. You need to be able to play in a key to suit their voice. Of course a great singer has great range, but even so they will prefer keys suited to their voice. Also, many instrumentals are typically played in a certain key. While it is easy to play the guitar in G, the same tune on a fiddle might usually be played in A.

The capo acts as a clamp that shortens the string length. It raises the pitch of each string by an equal amount. This is convenient because you can use the same chord shape you have already learned to play a higher-pitched chord. Or, you can play the melody from notes positions written for one key and use a capo to step the pitch up into a different key.

For each fret you move the capo up, the pitch is raised one half-step; for example, D becomes D-sharp (D#). Another way to think of this is that you are effectively moving the nut to a new location.

Tips for Using a Capo

- Place the capo directly over the fret– not behind it– to exert even pressure on the strings.
- Play chord shapes as though the capo is the nut location. For example, a C-chord for G tuning will be a D-chord when the capo is on the 2nd fret. See the chart. Think of the capo as using a finger to *barre* the fret. You are not changing where the notes are on the guitar fretboard.
- Use the chord numbering system (see page 28) to communicate chords to other players when you are using a capo. For example, instead of saying "I am playing a G chord, but my capo is on fret 2, so it is really an A chord." Just say "It is the I chord in the key of A." The other players then will know the right chord whether or not they are using a capo.
- Capos are not used much above the 7th fret, as it does not leave much room to play. As a start, learn to play in the keys of G, C and D and use a capo to play in other keys.

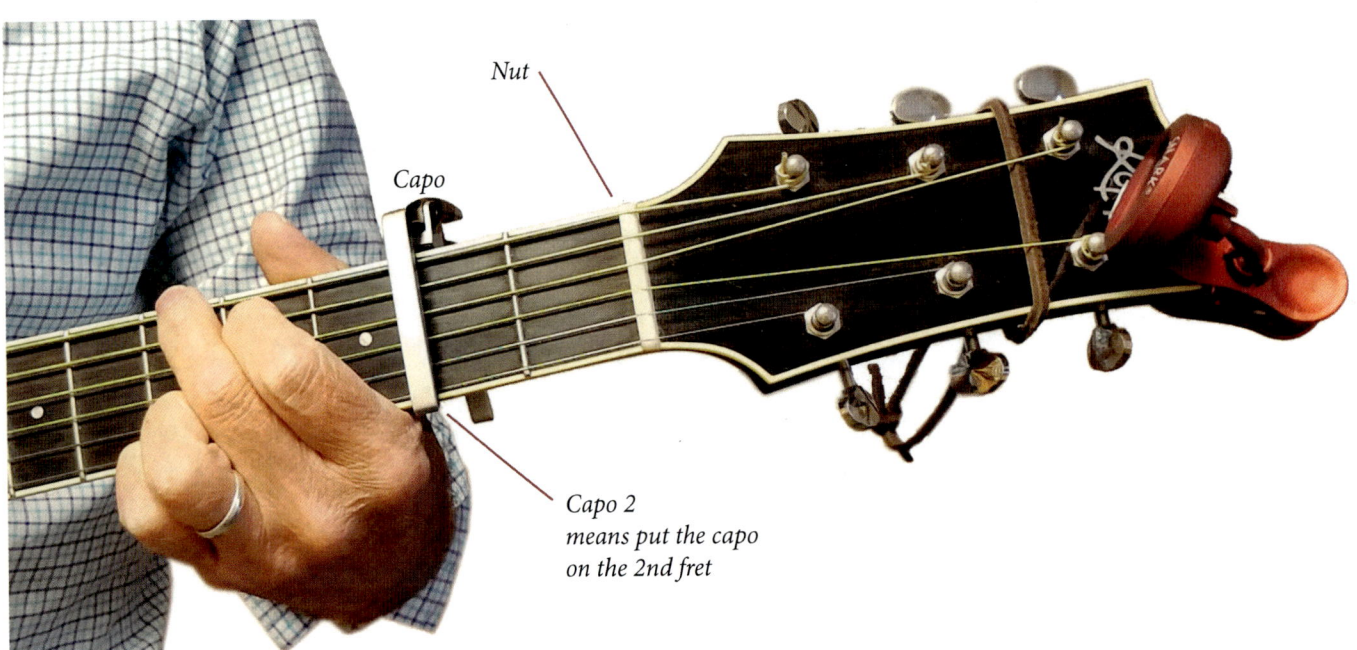

Nut

Capo

Capo 2 means put the capo on the 2nd fret

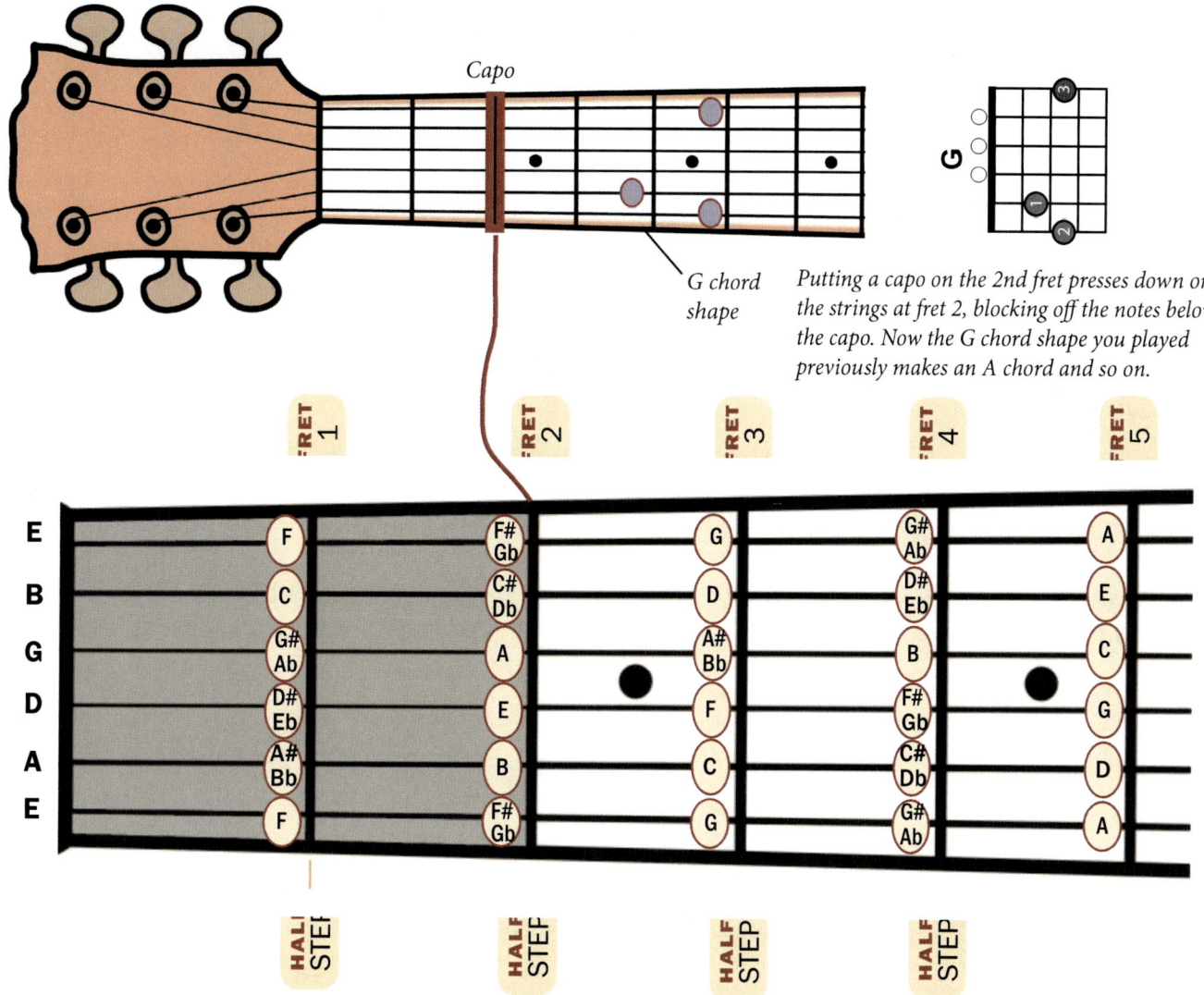

Capo

G chord shape

Putting a capo on the 2nd fret presses down on the strings at fret 2, blocking off the notes below the capo. Now the G chord shape you played previously makes an A chord and so on.

Guitar Capo Chart

Capo on Fret		0 (none)	1	2	3	4	5	6	7
Guitar Key		G	G#/Ab	A	A#/Bb	B	C	C#/Db	D
Common Chords	I	G	G#	A	Bb	B	C	C#	D
	IV	C	C#	D	Eb	E	F	F#	G
	V	D	D#	E	F	F#	G	G#	A

Playing a Slide

A distinctive sound in guitar playing is the slide. Sliding is a left-hand technique. In the next song you will learn to slide from the 2nd to the 5th fret on the D string.

On the D string (string 4), place the left-hand 2nd finger on the 2nd fret and pick that string with the thumb of the right hand. Let the note ring for a second. For a good slide sound, you must first hear the starting note. Next, move your hand and forearm to slide that 2nd finger up to the 5th fret while the tone is still sounding from that single pick of the string. You should be able to hear the pitch rise as you slide up the neck. Practice this 10 times in a row. Take your time sliding up; you don't have to move too fast. Stay in control and strive for a good tone.

Common Mistakes When Sliding

Moving the finger and not the hand and forearm. Keep your hand in the same shape and move your forearm and hand up the neck.

Pressing too hard with the left hand. It only takes a little pressure from the left-hand fingers to make a good-sounding note. If you press too hard, your finger and hand won't slide easily. Practice putting less pressure on the fretting finger before sliding up. Try this: Place your finger on the 2nd fret, but don't press down. Pick the string and slowly apply pressure until it sounds good. See how little pressure you can use to make a good clean sound. Using less pressure, your finger will slide easily up the string. This will also help keep your fingers from getting sore and your hand from getting tired while you play.

Stopping too soon. To get a clean sound, slide all the way to the fret with your finger pressed on the string before stopping the slide.

Practice sliding to get a smooth sound. Practice slow and fast slides. Try to keep the starting and ending notes of the slide in tempo, so that they are equal length. Don't forget to watch the videos that go with this book.

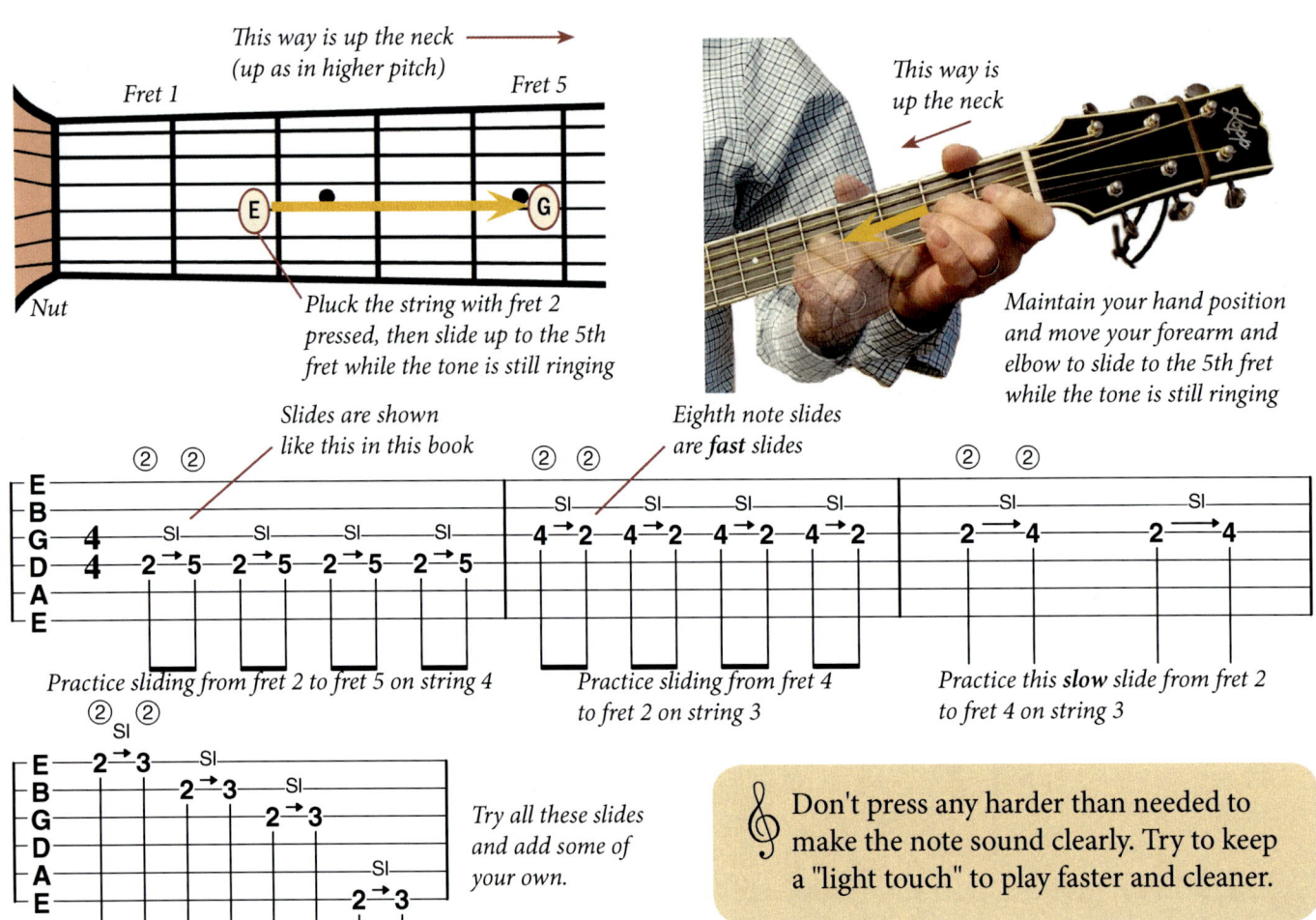

Will the Circle Be Unbroken Melody Guitar Tab

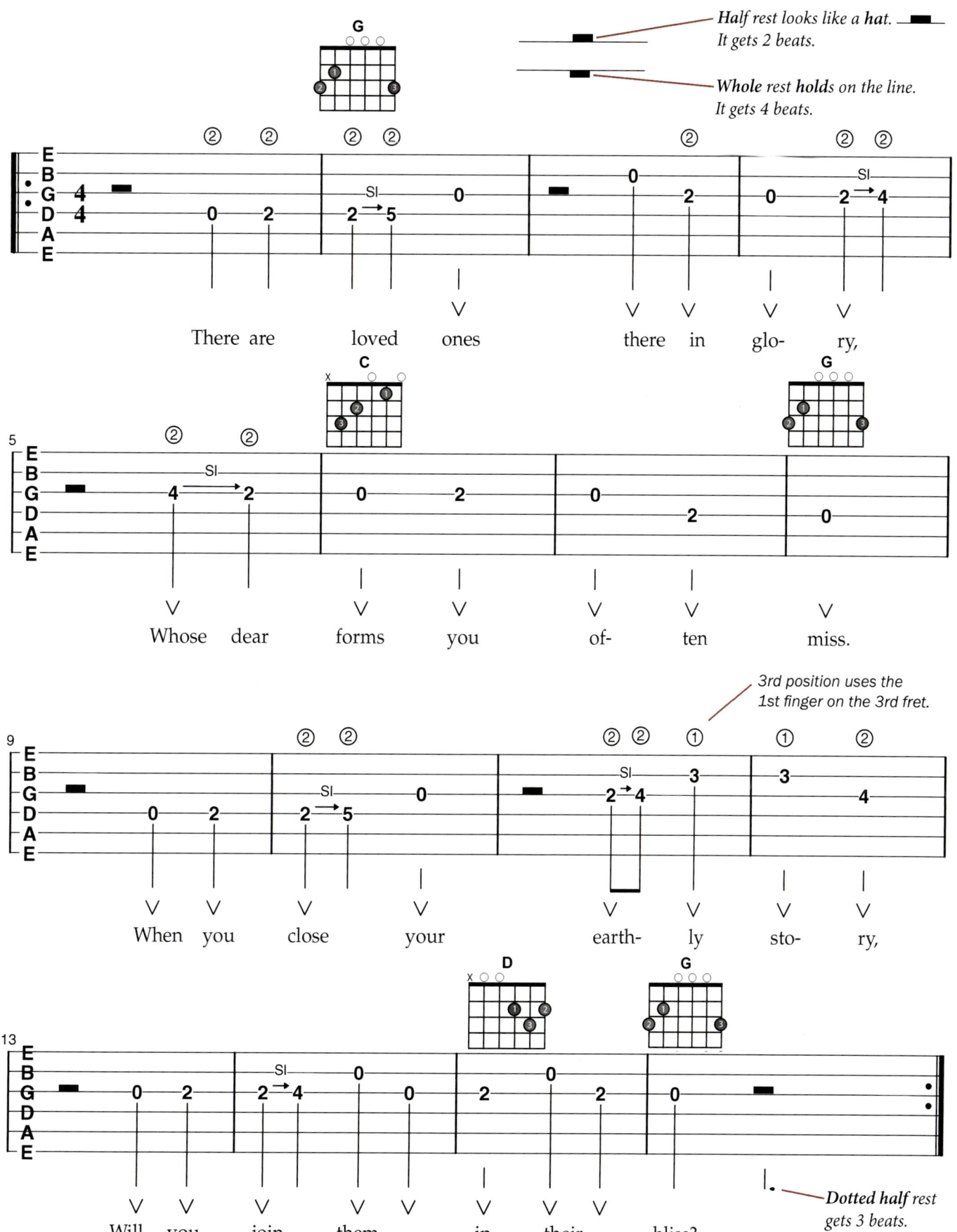

Will the Circle Be Unbroken Rhythm

This rhythm part mixes the pick/strum rhythm and adds walk-ups,walk-downs, and a slide to add interest to the backup part.

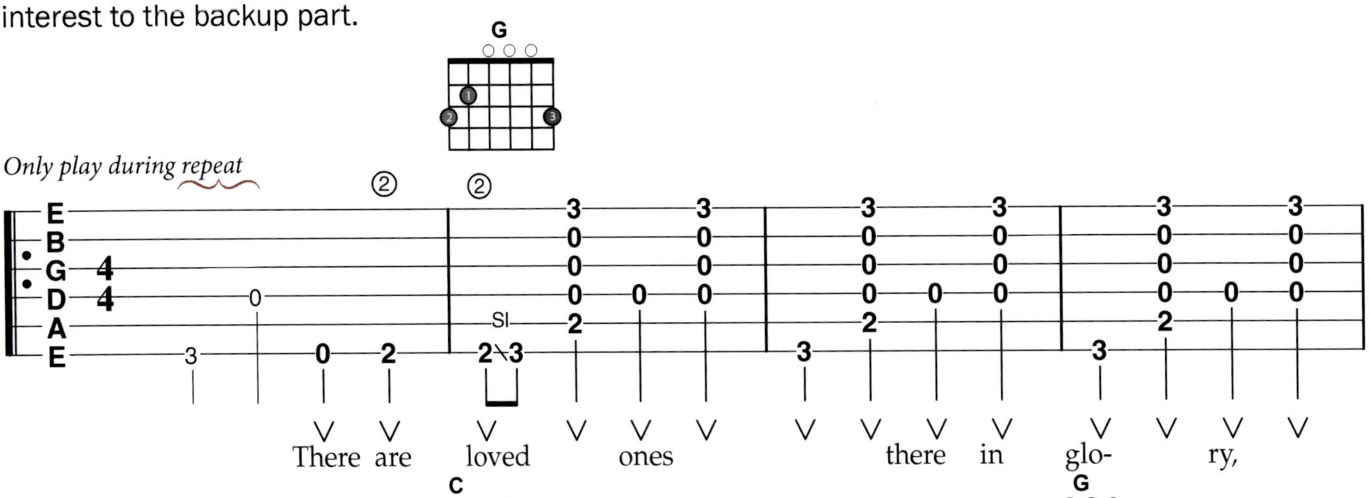

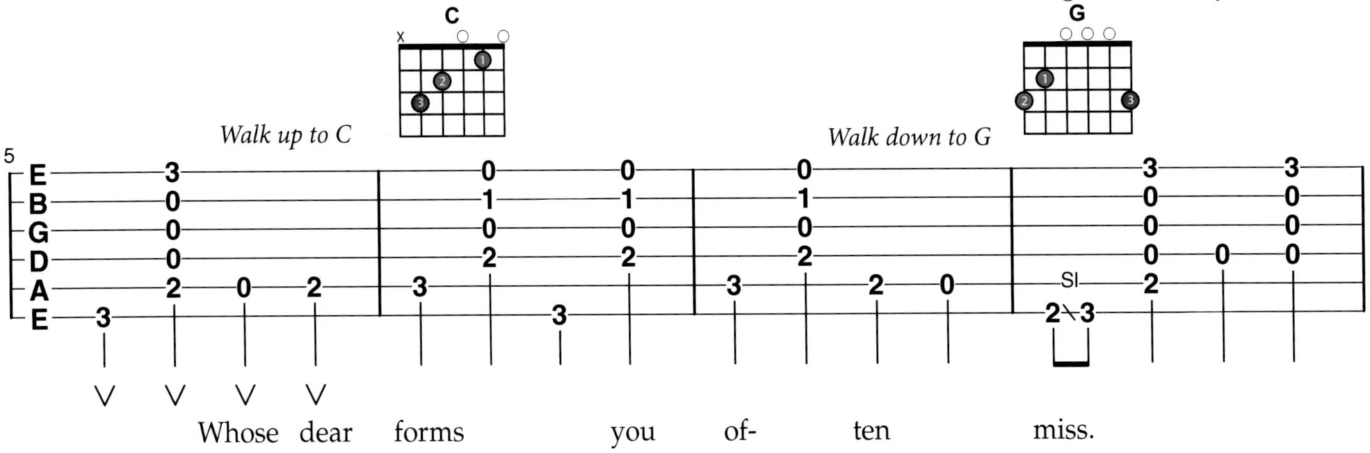

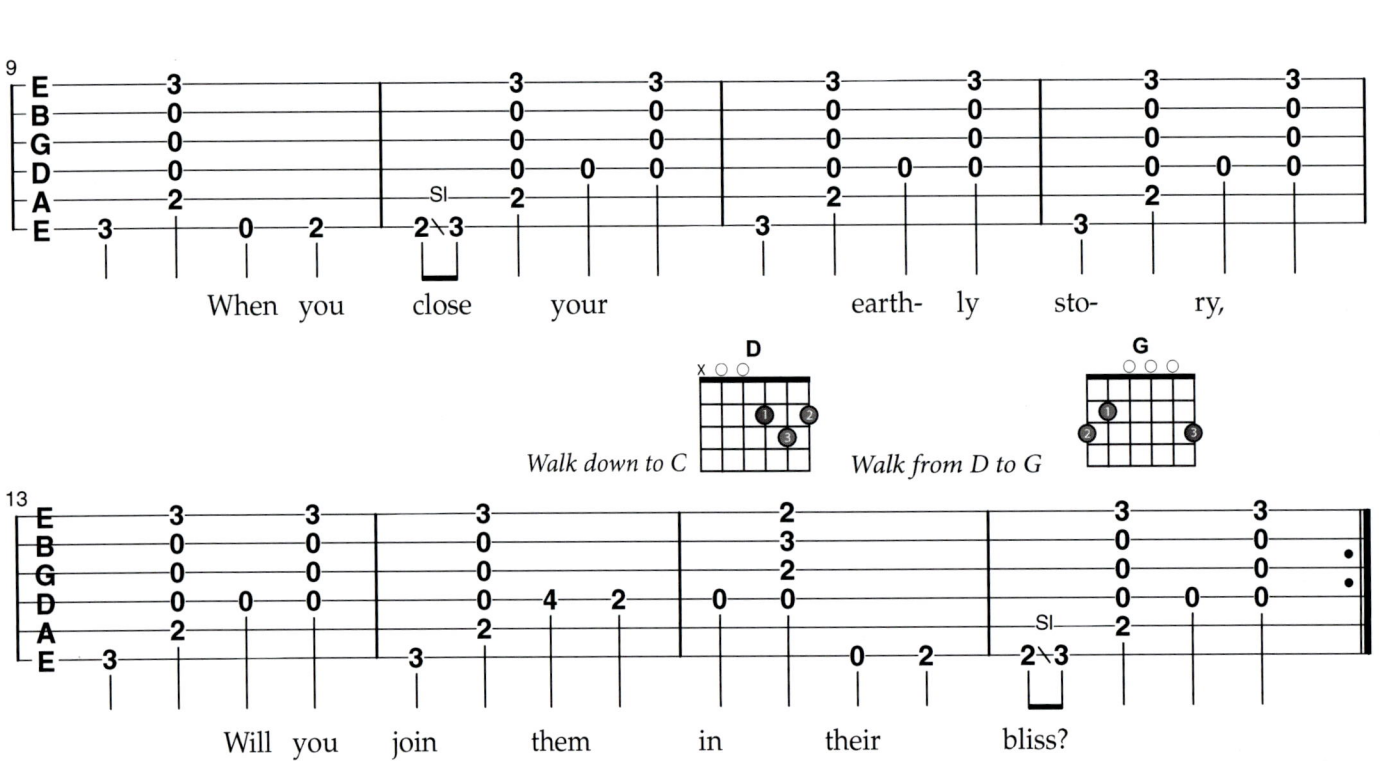

Will the Circle Be Unbroken Lyrics

The original lyrics to Will the Circle Be Unbroken were written in 1907 by Ada R. Habershorn for music composed by Charles H. Gabriel. Since that time it has been adapted as a bluegrass standard and various newer lyrics are sung. You can look up versions by the Carter Family and others.

G (I)
There are loved ones there in glory,
G (I)   C (iv)   G (I)
Whose dear forms you often miss.
G (I)
When you close your earthly story,
G (I)   D (V)   G (I)
Will you join them in their bliss?

Chorus
Will the circle be unbroken
By and by, Lord, by and by?
Is a better home awaiting
In the sky, Lord, in the sky?

You remember songs of heaven,
Which you sang with childish voice.
Do you love the hymns they taught you,
Or are songs of Earth your choice?
    Repeat Chorus

You can picture happy gath'rings,
Round the fireside long ago,
And you think of tearful partings,
When they left you here below.
    Repeat Chorus

One by one their seats were emptied,
One by one they went away.
Now the family is parted,
Will it be complete one day?
    Repeat Chorus

Bluegrass Lyrics

The roots of many bluegrass songs are from much older songs of the British Isles. When the songs arrived in Appalachia, lyrics were adapted to appeal to the lives of ordinary people; for example the song, Lord Randal becomes plain old Jimmy Randall.

American Version
*Where have you been, Jimmy Randall, my son,
Where have you been, my handsome young one?
I've been to my true love, Mama, (twice)
Make my bed, Mama, I'm sick to my grave.*

English Lyrics
*Where ha' ye been, Lord Randal, my son?
Where ha' ye been, my handsome young man?
I met wi' my true-love; mother, mak my bed soon,
For I'm wearied wi huntin, an fain wad lie down.*

Often, traditional songs have what are referred to as *floating lyrics*. These work well in any number of songs and show up over and over. One example is:

*Wish I had a needle and thread
As fine as I could sew,
I'd sew my true love to my back
And down the road I'd go.*

This verse appears in Late Last Night in this book, It is also often used in these songs: Shady Grove, Run Mountain, Boil Them Cabbage Down, and many more. So, when you can't remember the lyrics, just throw in a few floating verses or make up something of your own. Folk music is music of the people. Contribute your own twist; it belongs to you too!

Playing a Pull-Off

Another item in your bag of guitar sounds is the pull-off. Pull-offs are a left-hand technique. For a pull-off, you start the sound with a fretted note picked with the right hand, and then end on a lower note. The ending note can be an open string or a note fretted with a different finger. Let the first note sound, and then pluck the string with the left-hand finger moving toward your palm as you pull it off the string. The goal is to produce two separate but connected tones.

In Walking Cane you are going to use a pull-off from the 2nd fret of the D string to the open D string. You will pick the string once with the right-hand thumb for the E note and then pluck it with the left-hand finger as you pull that finger off the string. You should hear both the E and D notes evenly. Try using the tip of the left finger, just before the nail, to pluck the pull-off.

Practice pulling your finger from fret 2 to the open string sound. Pluck the string with your left hand as you pull the finger off the string toward your palm.

Practice pulling your finger from fret 2 to the open D-string sound. Remember, pick the string just once with the right hand and pull-off the left hand finger to pluck the other note.

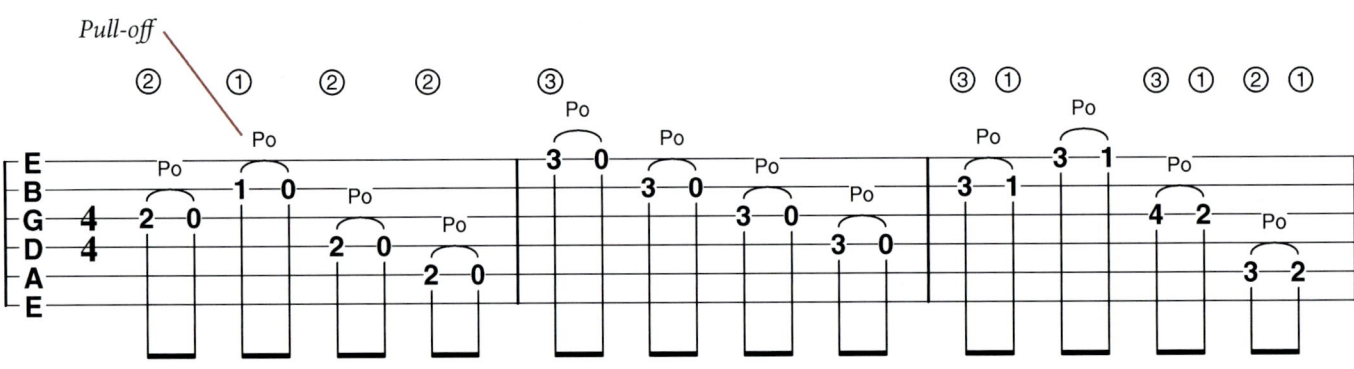

Try pull-offs to open strings as shown here.

Here are more pull-offs to practice.

Harmonics

To play a *harmonic*, lightly touch the strings at the 12th fret and strum. Don't press them down. You are using your finger to shorten the string length to create the harmonic sound.

To play the harmonic:

- Place your left index or middle finger directly over the fret. In this case we will use the 12th fret. The 7th and 5th frets also produce harmonic tones.
- Do not press down, instead, lightly touch your ring finger to all the strings. Strum down once and then remove your finger from the fret.
- You should hear a bell-like tone.

12th fret

Touch lightly and quickly remove finger from frets after strumming

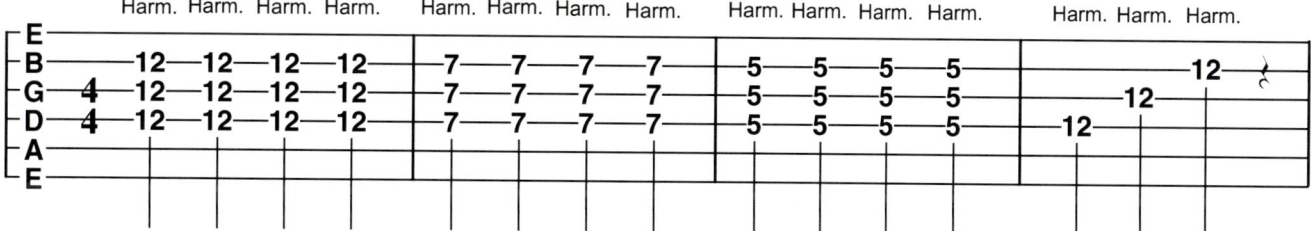

G Run with Slide, Pull-off, and Harmonic

Here is a G run often heard in bluegrass that you can use as a fill-in or at the end of a song to put it all together for a polished sound.

Practice each group of notes until you have it down smoothly, then put it all together.

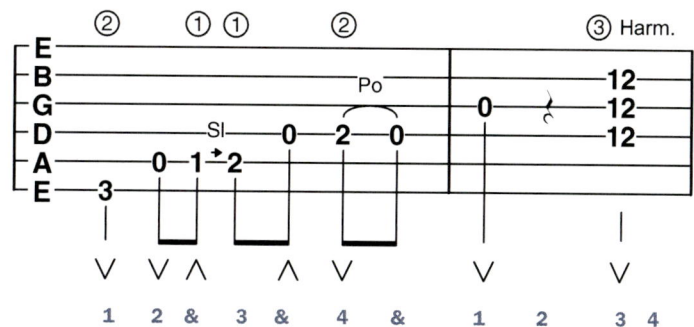

Giving the Count

To coordinate the tempo for a group of players, the leader for the song "counts in" to let the other players know how fast to play the beats in each measure. For a song in 4/4 time, you count "1 2 3 4" or "1 and 2 and 3 and 4 and," to break it down further. Before you count out loud, hum a bit of the song to yourself to decide the speed you want it played, then tap your foot to that beat, and finally count out loud with that beat. Be ready to start on time with that tempo and on the correct beat; in this case beat 3.

Hand Me Down My Walking Cane Rhythm Guitar Tab

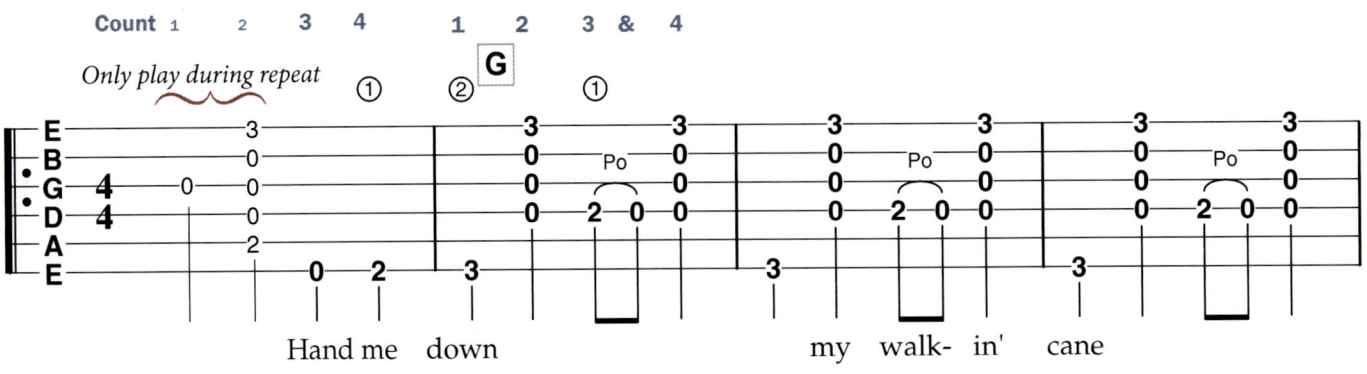
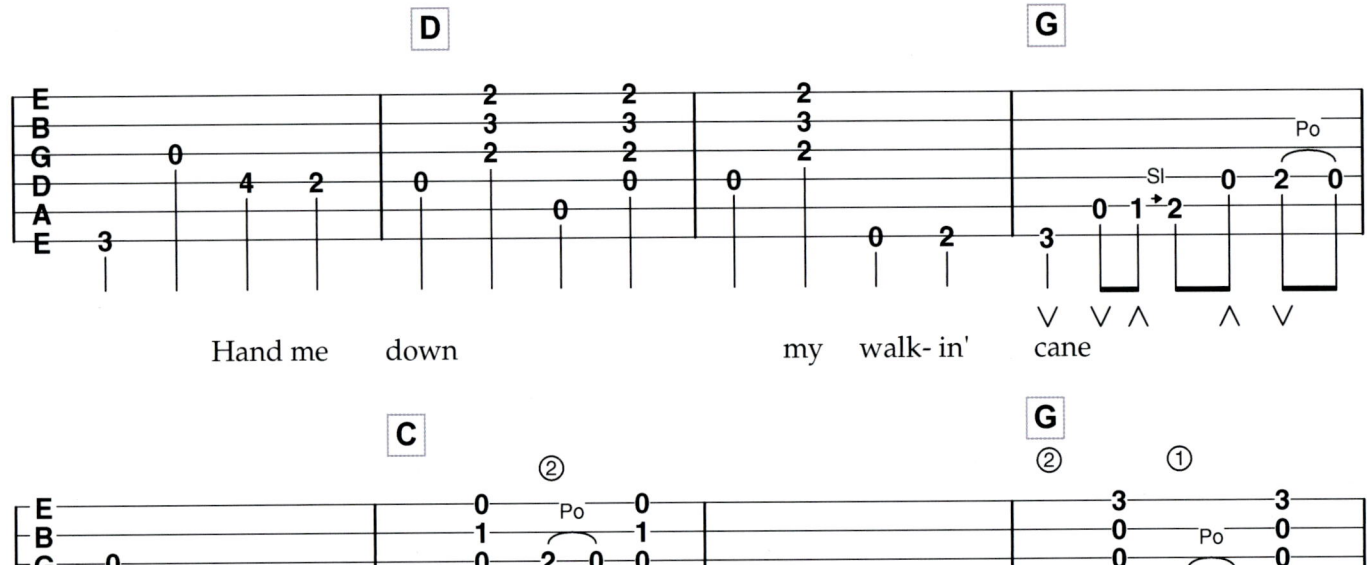
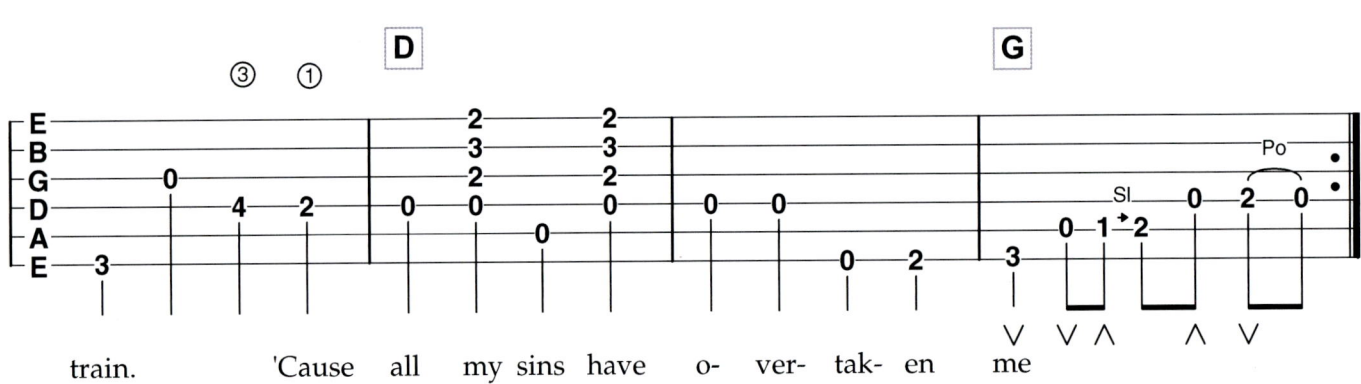

Hand Me Down My Walking Cane Melody Guitar Tab

This song starts on beat 3 and 4. These are called "pick-up" notes. The downbeat is in the second measure. The count is: 1, 2, 3, 4, 1, 2, then come in on beat 3.

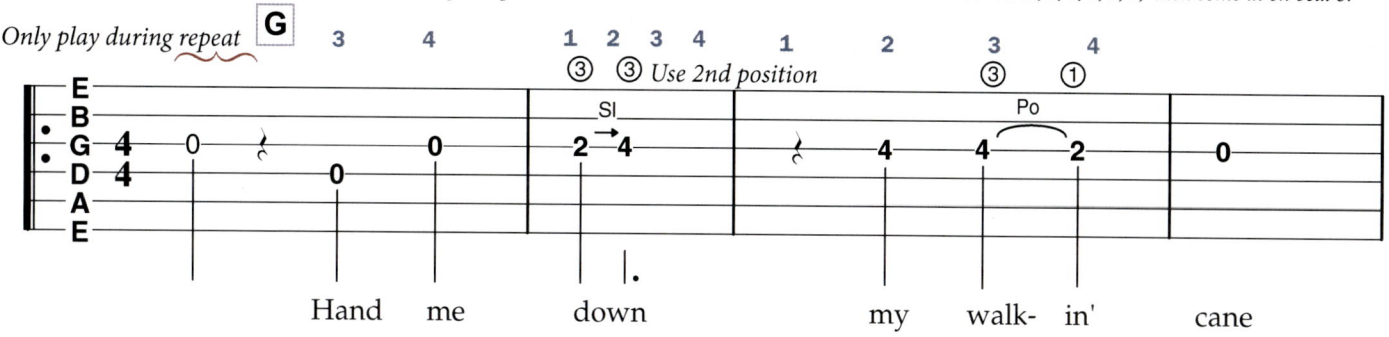

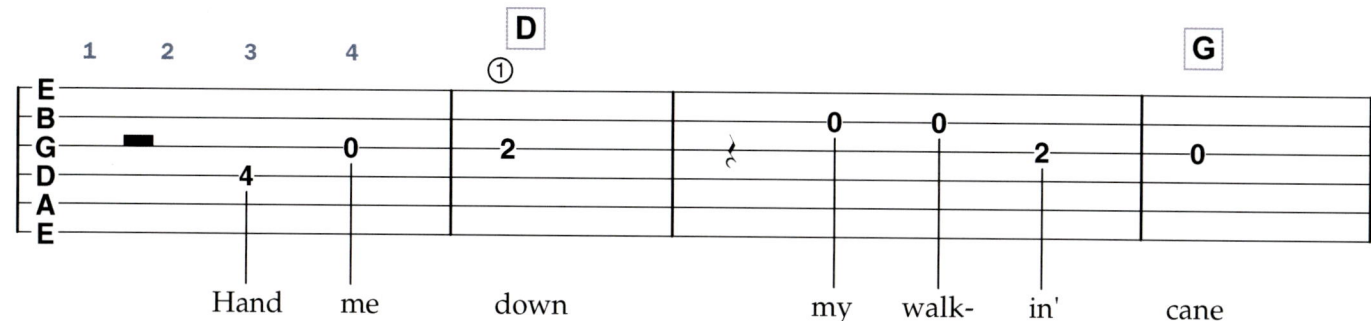

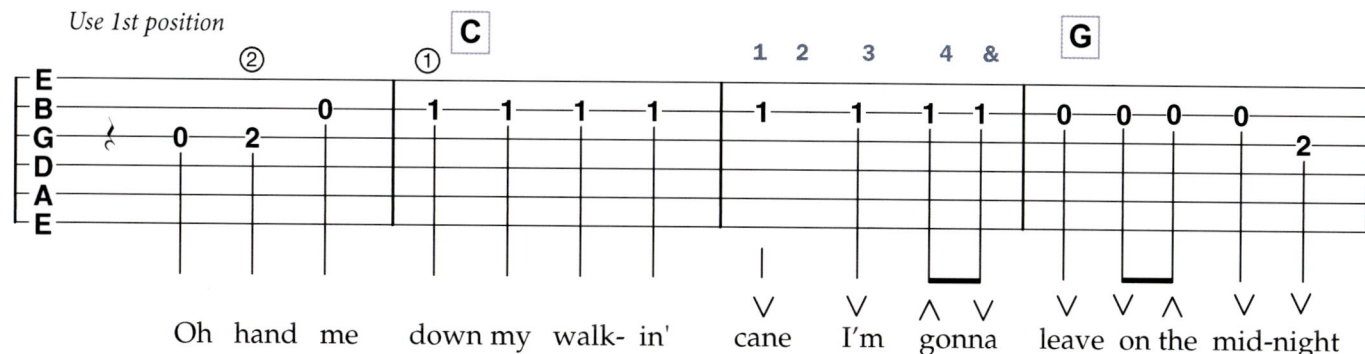

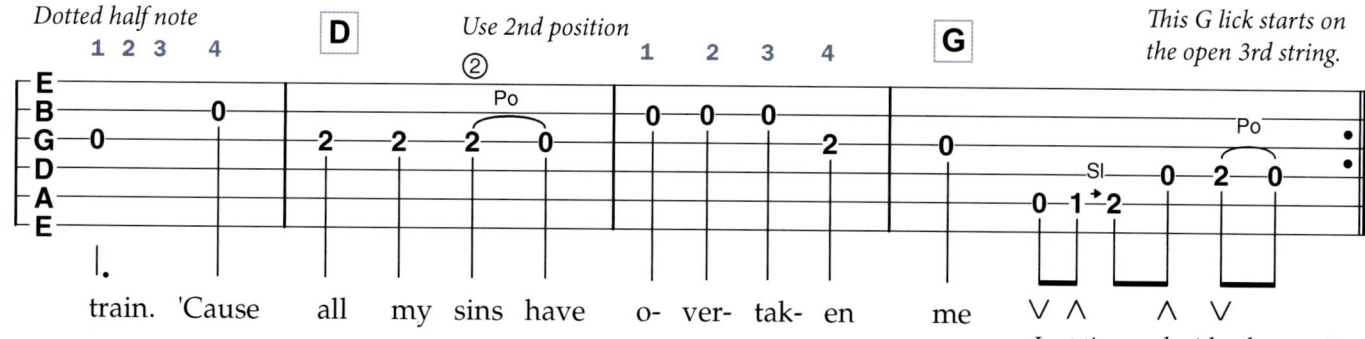

Last time end with a harmonic after this G-lick.

More verses

Hand me down my bottle of corn, (x 3)
I'm gonna get drunk as sure as you're born
'Cause all my sins they have overtaken me

I got drunk and landed in jail (x 3)
Got nobody to go my bail.
'Cause all my sins ... me.

Devil chased me 'round a stump. (x 3)
Thought he'd catch me with every jump.
'Cause all my sins ... me.

If I die in Tennessee (x 3)
Ship me back by C.O.D.
'Cause all my sins ... me.

Playing a Hammer-on

Hammer-ons are another left-hand technique. Practice a basic hammer-on from the open string to the 2nd fret on the D string, which moves the sound from D to E. Using the D string (string 4), first pick the open string with the thumb of the right hand. Let the note ring for just a second. For a good hammer-on sound, you must first hear the starting note. Then, hammer on the 2nd finger on the 2nd fret, while the tone is still sounding from that single pick of the string. You should be able to hear the pitch rise to the new note. Take your time adding the hammer; it doesn't have to be fast at first. Stay in control and strive for a good tone, gradually increasing your speed as you gain confidence.

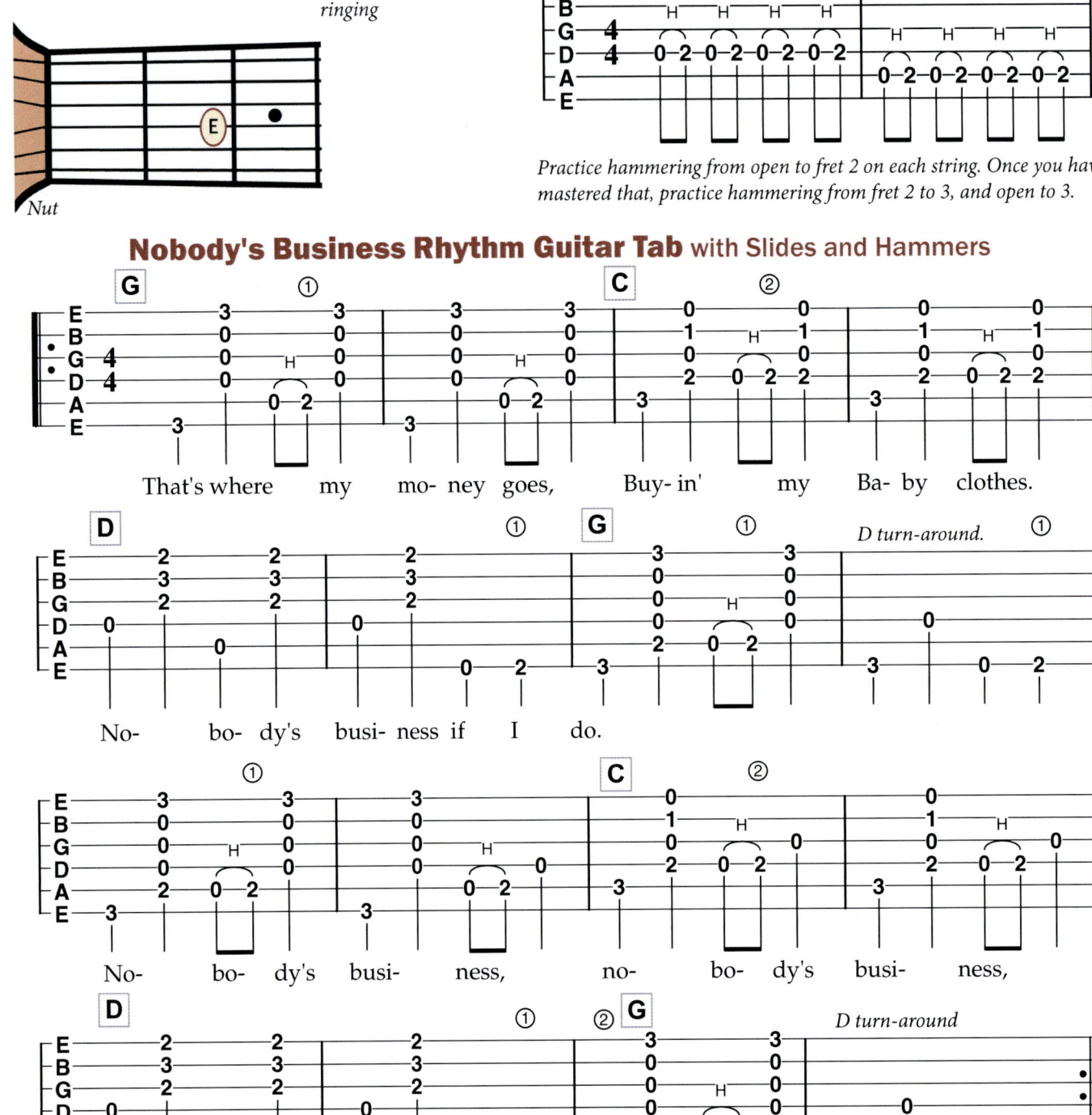

Practice hammering from open to fret 2 on each string. Once you have mastered that, practice hammering from fret 2 to 3, and open to 3.

Nobody's Business Rhythm Guitar Tab with Slides and Hammers

Nobody's Business Melody Guitar Tab

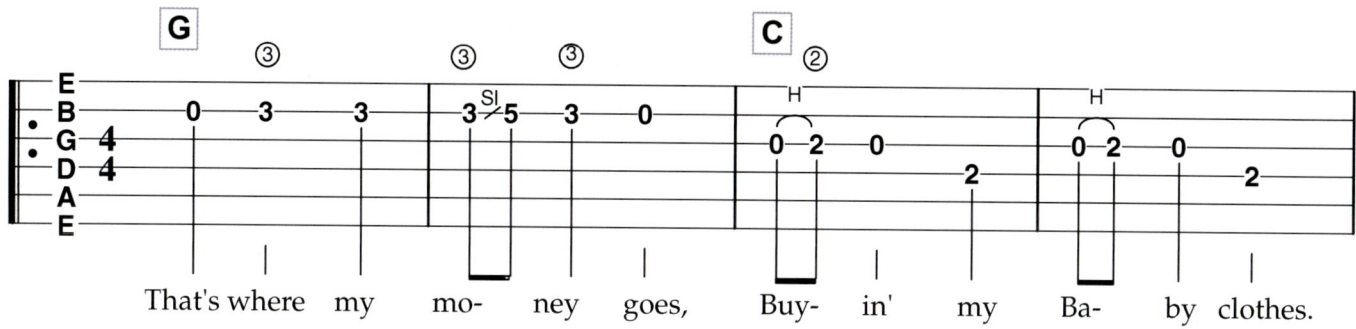
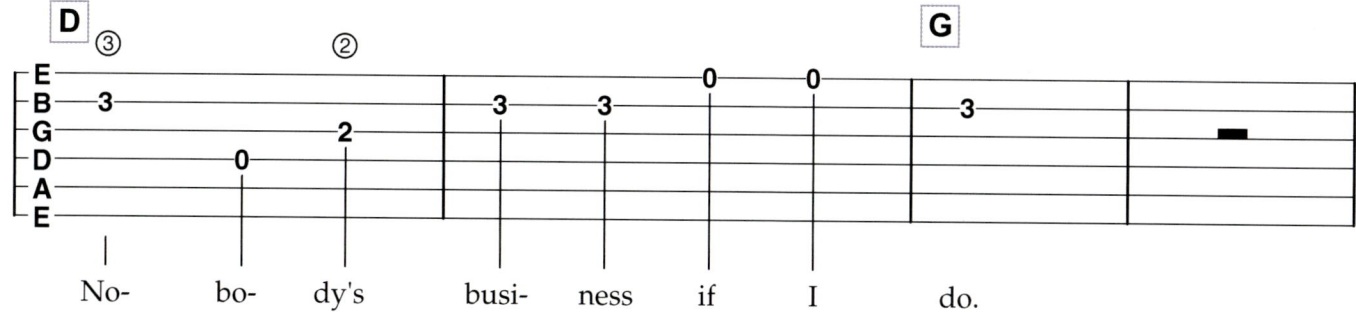
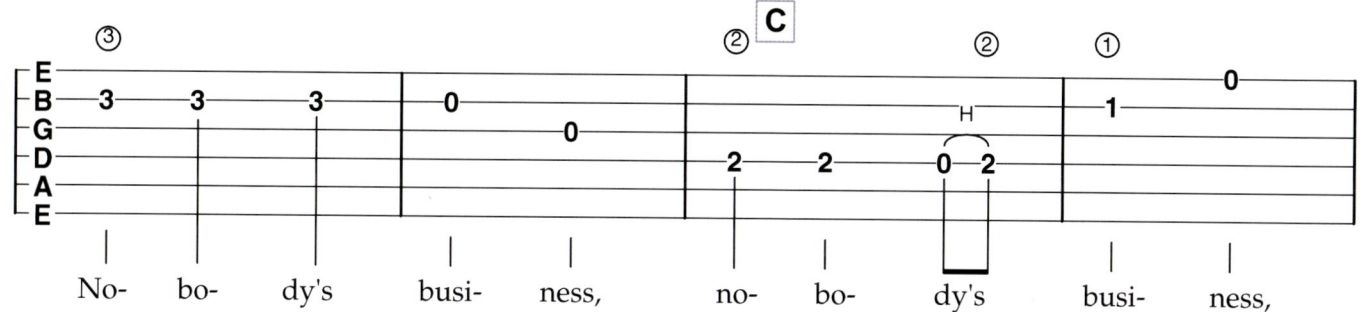
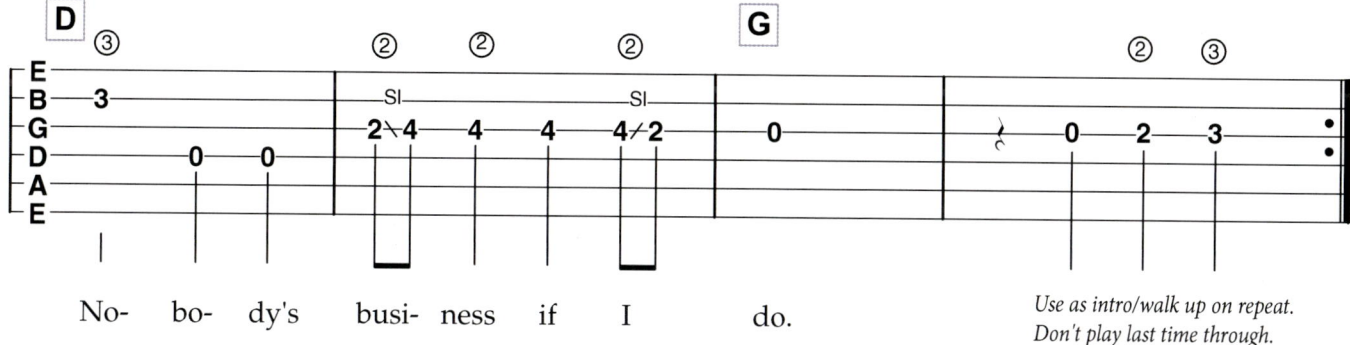

More verses

G (I)　　　　　　　C (IV)
Sometimes I ramble, I get drunk and gamble.
　　D (V)　　　　　　　　　G (I)
It's nobody's business if I do,
　　　　　　　　C (IV)
Nobody's business, it's nobody's business,
　　D (V)　　　　　G (I)
It's nobody's business if I do.

Morphine's gonna run me crazy. Cocaine's gonna kill me baby.
Cigarettes gonna cause me to lose my mind...

She drives a limousine, and I buy her gasoline.
It's nobody's business if I do...

Cold pork and pickled feet, bacon and sausage meat,
Nobody's business what I eat...

Chord Numbering

One of the skills for playing by "ear" is to learn to recognize the chords in any key. Every major scale uses the same pattern of whole and half steps, so the fourth is always going to be the same number of half steps above the root (the I chord) regardless of the key. If you listen for the relative change in pitch, the only difference between the keys is the starting tone.

Key	I	WHOLE STEP → ii	WHOLE STEP → iii	HALF STEP → IV	WHOLE STEP → V	WHOLE STEP → vi	WHOLE STEP → VII°	HALF STEP → VIII (i)
C	C	D	E	F	G	A	B	C
D	D	E	F#	G	A	B	C#	D
G	G	A	B	C	D	E	F#	G

The I, IV, and V chords are the most used in any key (for example G, C, and D in the key of G). Many songs start on the I chord of the key, but not all. Our next song, *Late Last Night*, starts on the IV chord. Listen to the walk-up notes that start the song, they are the 1, 2, and 3 of the scale and then land on the 4th tone of the scale. The song usually "resolves" or ends on the I chord, of the key, which is G in this song.

Playing an Intro/Turnaround/Ending Lick

Speaking of those walk-up notes, the start of the song is an important part. It sets the tempo and tone for the song, and makes it sound polished. Here are some tips:

- play an intro to set the tempo for the song and start you in.
- play a turn-around, this musically takes you back to the beginning of the song, it is often the last 4 measures of the song.
- play an ending to polish off the song and let your audience know it is time to clap!

Guit-Jo Jo Intro

Fiddle players call these introductory beats "potatoes", "taters", or "spuds". They are based on the rhythm *"po— ta- toes"*, with long *"po—"* and short *"ta-"* and *"toes"*. Since this is a guitar book, let's call them "guit-jo jos." Try this intro to set the tempo and launch into Late Last Night.

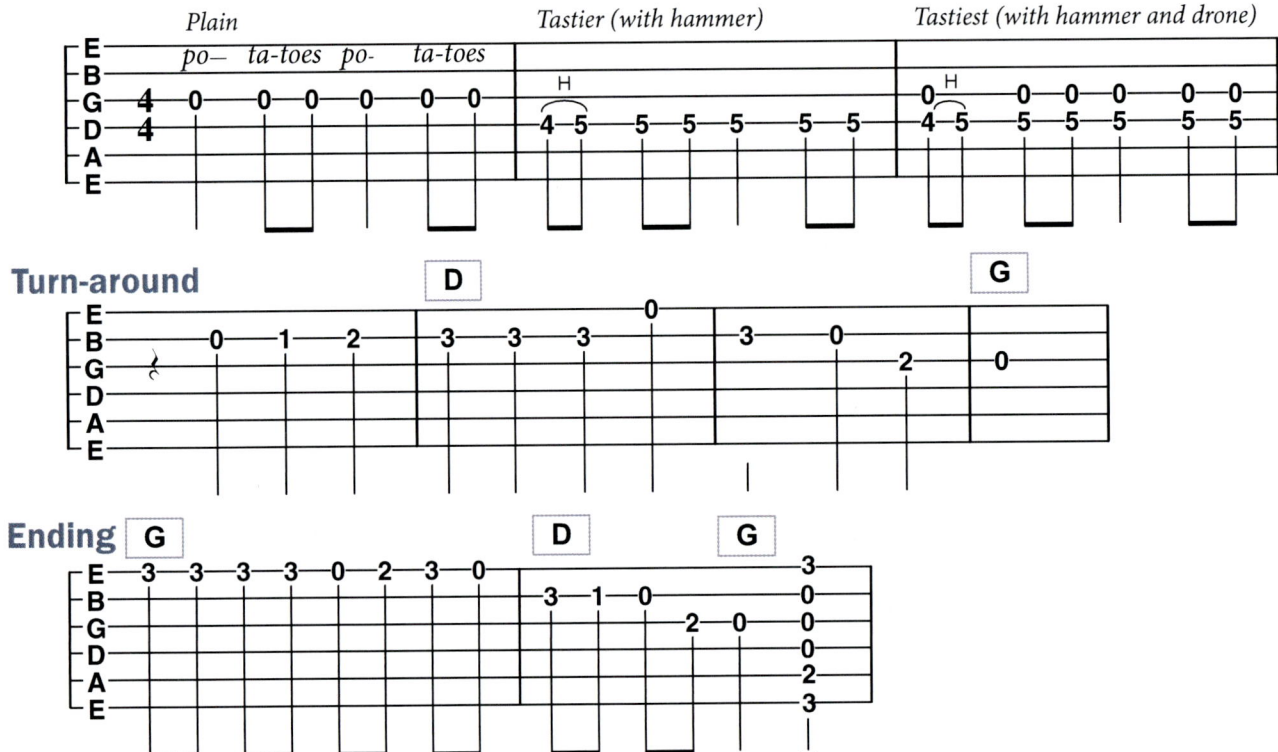

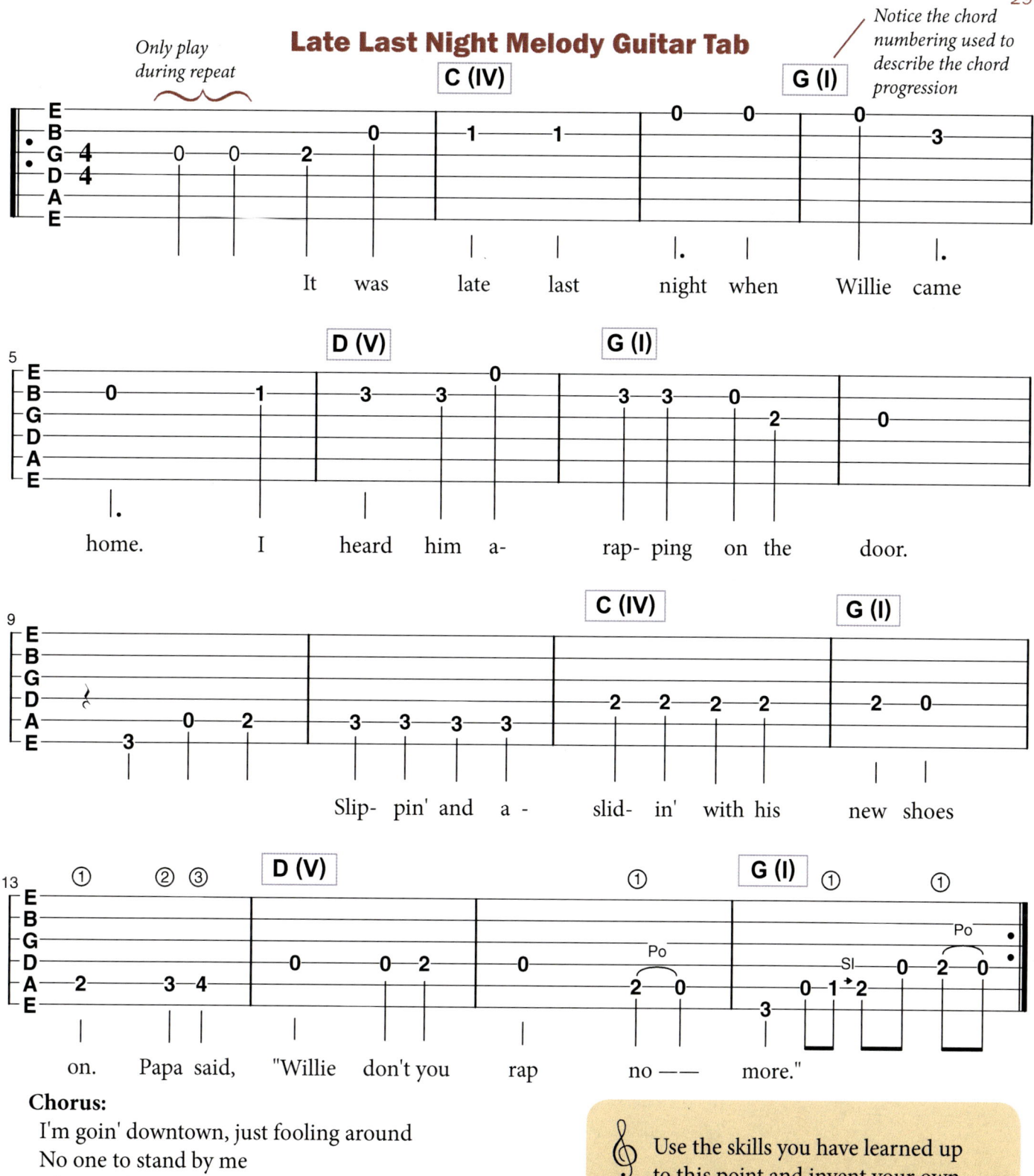

Chorus:
I'm goin' downtown, just fooling around
No one to stand by me
Oh me, oh my
What's gonna become of me

Use the skills you have learned up to this point and invent your own rhythm part for this song.

More verses

One old shirt is about all I've got
And a dollar is all I crave
Brought nothing with me into this world
Gonna take nothing to my grave

Wish I was down in old Baltimore
Sitting in an easy chair
One arm around my old guitar
And the other around my dear

Wish I had a needle and thread
As fine as I could sew
Sew them pretty girls to my back
And down the road I'd go

John Henry Rhythm Guitar Tab

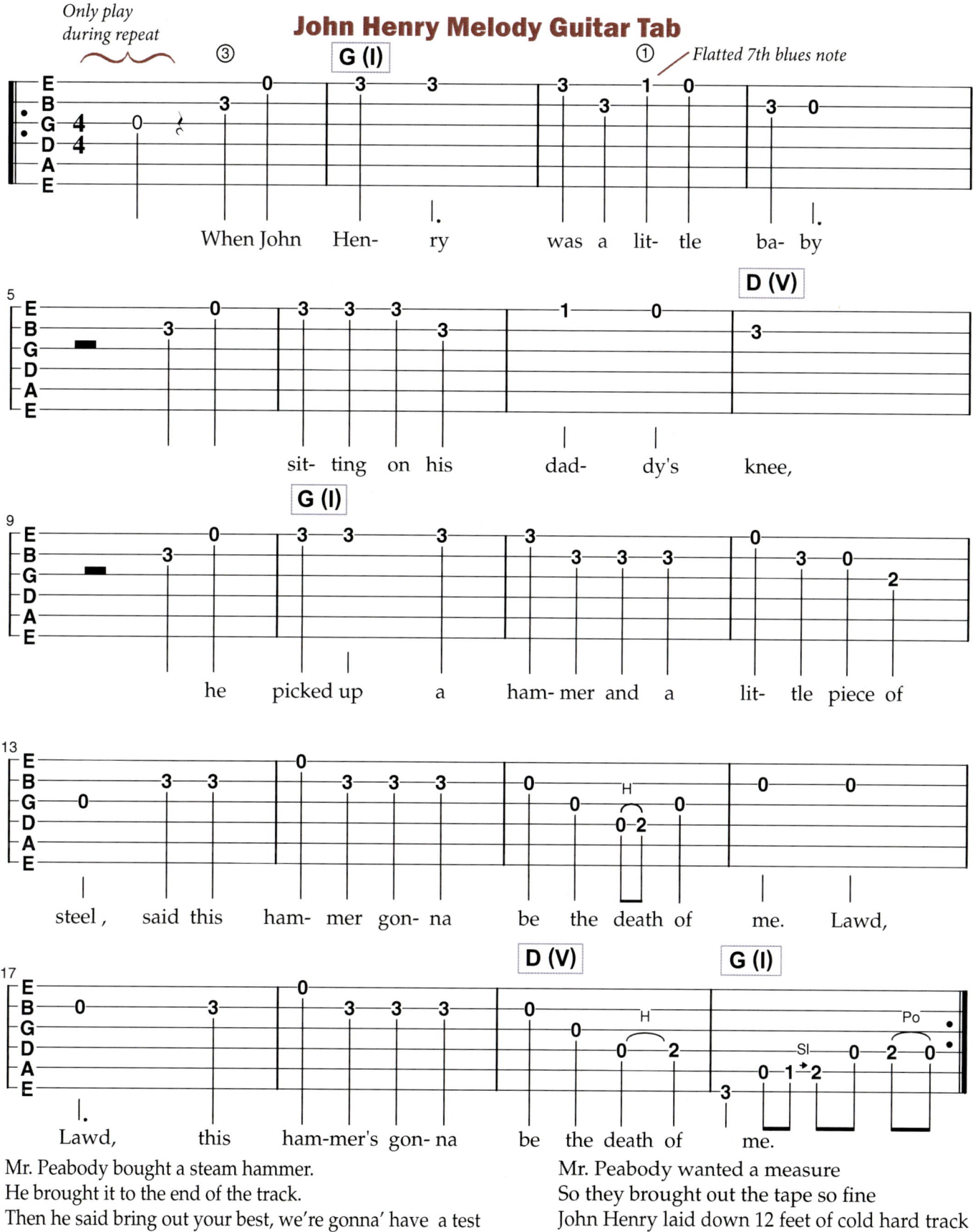

Mr. Peabody bought a steam hammer.
He brought it to the end of the track.
Then he said bring out your best, we're gonna' have a test
And if my hammer wins the rest of you can pack

John Henry went to the tunnel to drive
His hammer was by his side
He said before I would let that steam-hammer beat me down
You know I'll lay down this hammer and die

Mr. Peabody wanted a measure
So they brought out the tape so fine
John Henry laid down 12 feet of cold hard track
They tell me that the hammer just laid 9

John Henry had a sweet little wife
Her name was Polly Ann
When Johnny got sick and had to go to bed
Polly drove that steel just like a man

Movable F-Shape Chord

The F-shape chord can be moved up the guitar neck to produce different chords using the same shape. Use the F-shape chord for F, G, and D for playing rhythm on Little Maggie. Practice moving this chord shape to the 3rd, 5th and 12th frets for this song. Move your 3rd finger to the next string for the bass notes.

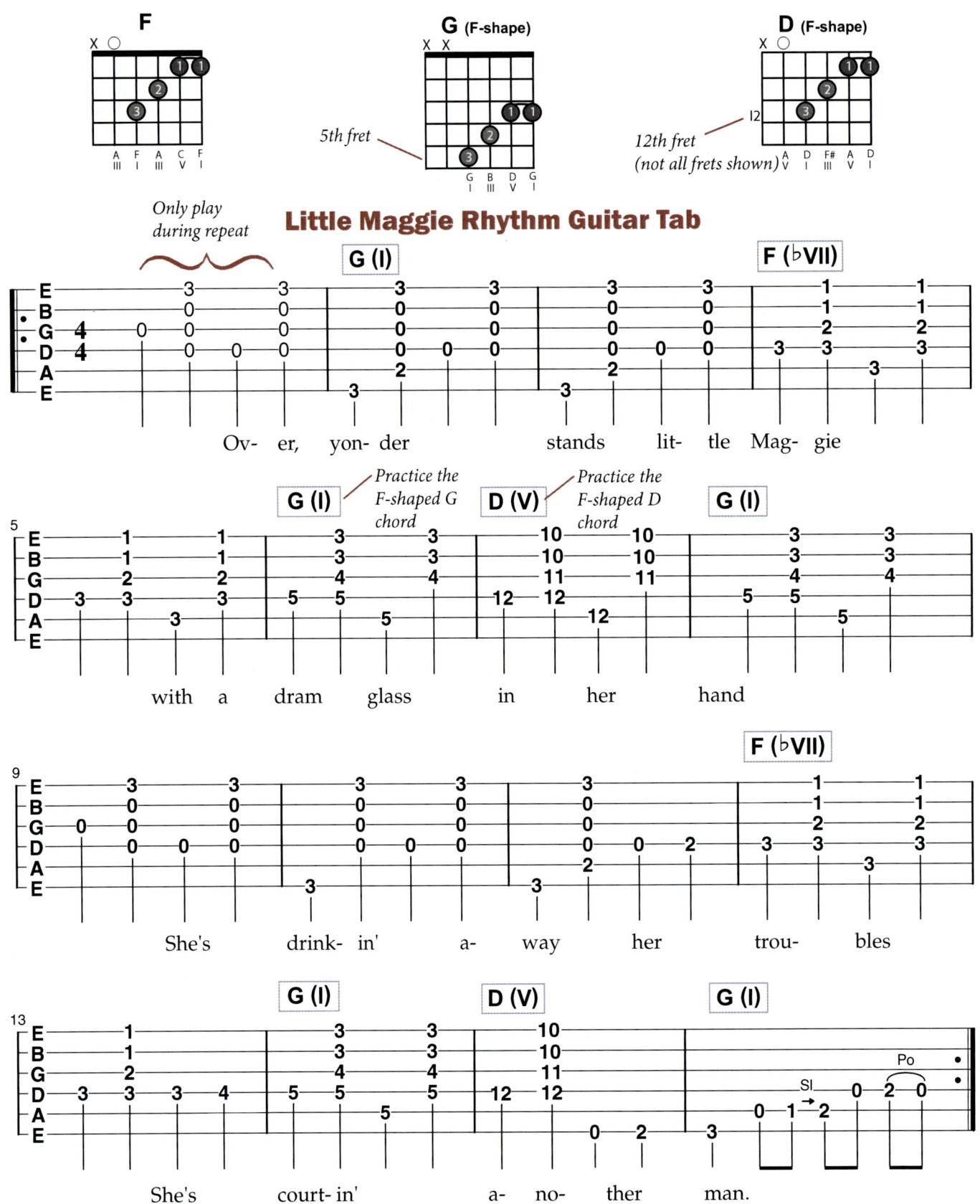

Little Maggie Melody Guitar Tab

Only play during repeat

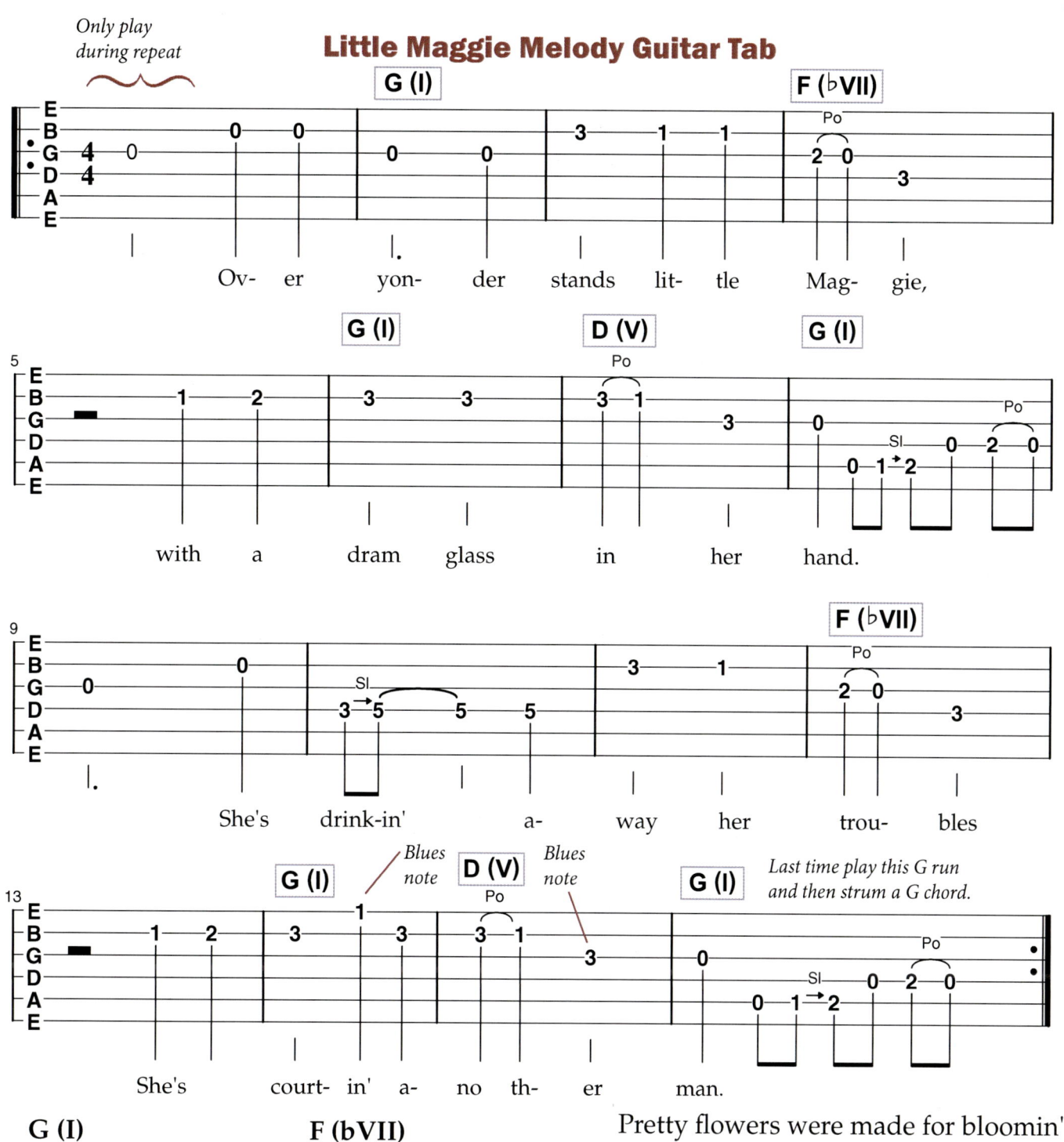

(Tab notation with lyrics:)

Ov- er yon- der stands lit- tle Mag- gie,
with a dram glass in her hand.
She's drink-in' a- way her trou- bles
She's court- in' a- no- th- er man.

Last time play this G run and then strum a G chord.

G (I)   **F (bVII)**
Last time I saw little Maggie
G (I)   **D (V)**   **G (1)**
She was sittin' on the banks of the sea
G   **F (bVII)**
With a forty-four all around her
G (I)   **D (V)**   **G (I)**
And a guitar on her knee.

Pretty flowers were made for bloomin'
Pretty stars were made to shine
Pretty women were made for lovin'
Little Maggie was made for mine.

Lay down your last gold dollar
Lay down your gold watch and chain
Little Maggie's gonna dance for daddy
Listen to that ol' guitar ring.

Go away, go away, little Maggie
Go and do the best you can
I'll get me another woman
You can get you another man.

> This new chord progression is: I, flat VII, I, V, I (G, F, G, D, G). The flat VII is common in bluegrass.

33

Playing in 3/4 Time

Down in the Willow Garden is in waltz time. Each measure gets 3 beats, with the strong beat on **1** while 2 and 3 are quieter, but still even in time. This arrangement uses different rhythm on the A, B, and C parts.

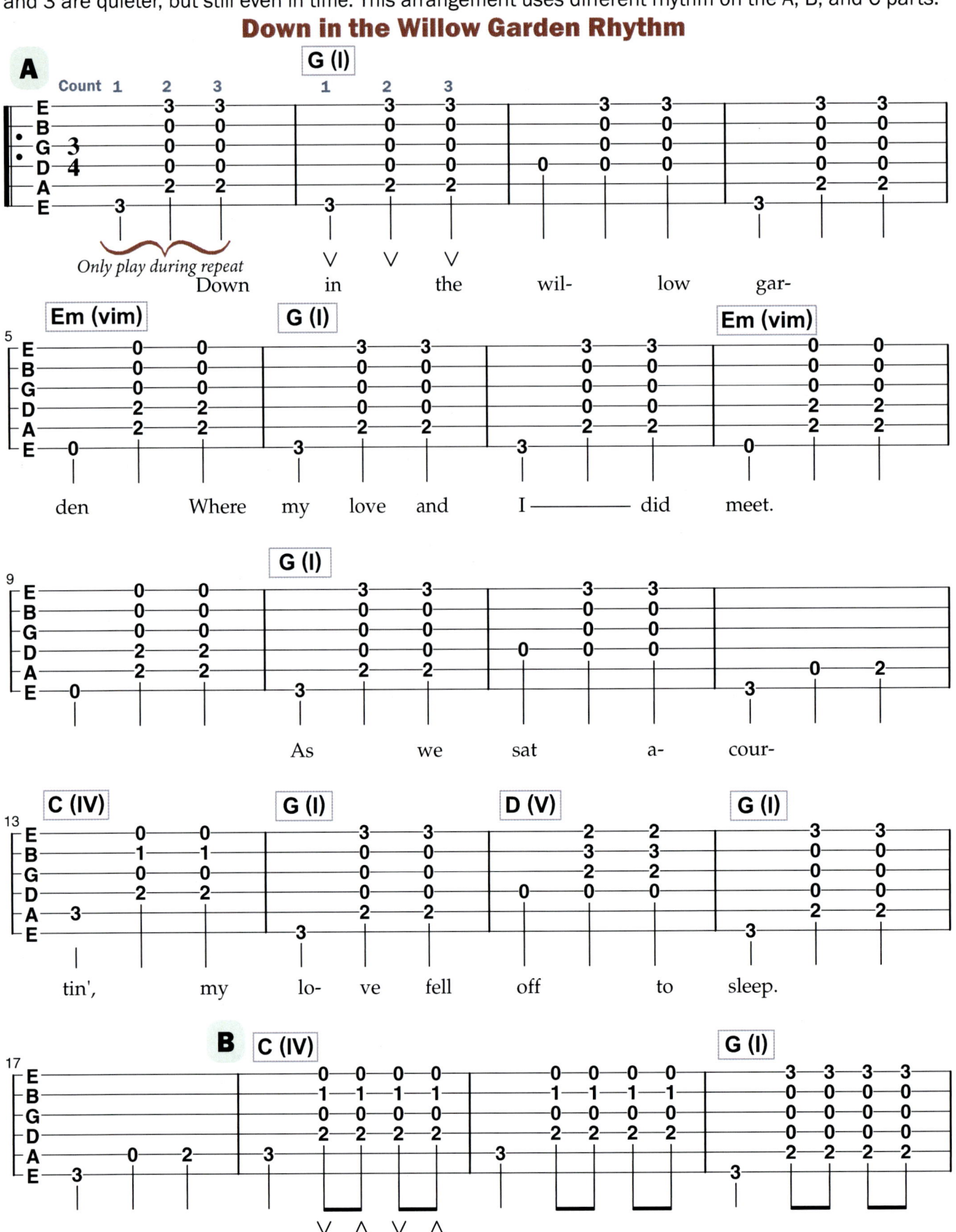

Down in the Willow Garden Rhythm

E Minor Chord

The relative minor chord in a key is formed from the 6th tone of the scale. Em is the relative minor in the key of G. See Playing Minor Chords on page 38 for more information.

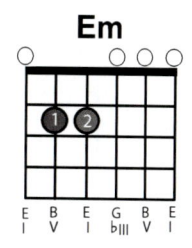

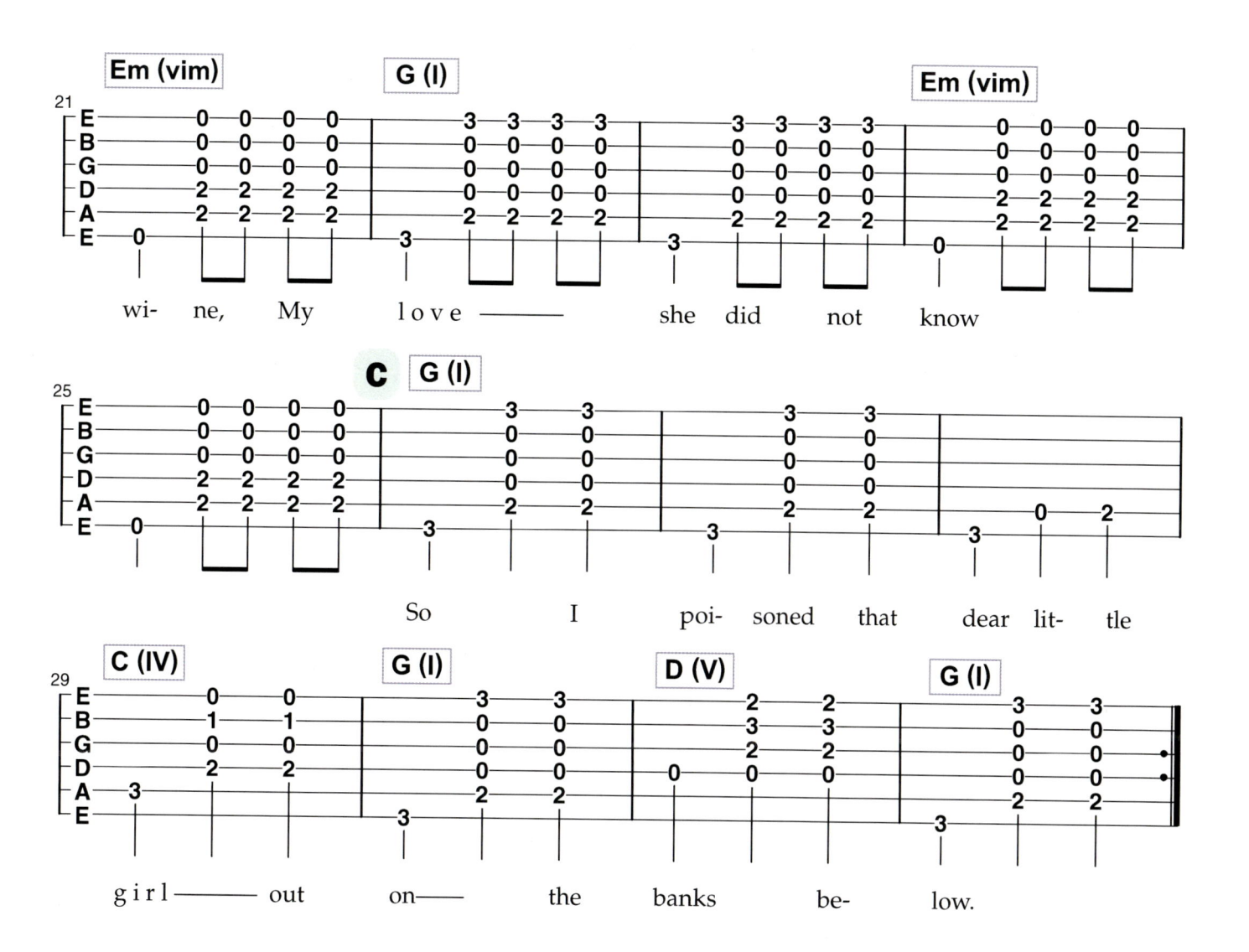

Em

Lyrics with chords:

Em (vim)	G (I)		Em (vim)
wi- ne, My	love	she did	not know

	G (I)		
	So I	poi- soned that	dear lit- tle

C (IV)	G (I)	D (V)	G (I)
girl out	on	the banks	be- low.

> It often works well to stick to one strum pattern for the verse. The song builds by varying the patterns Segmenting the song and using a distinctive pattern to bring out each part, making the verse and chorus different for example, steps up your playing to the next level.

Down in the Willow Garden Melody Guitar Tab

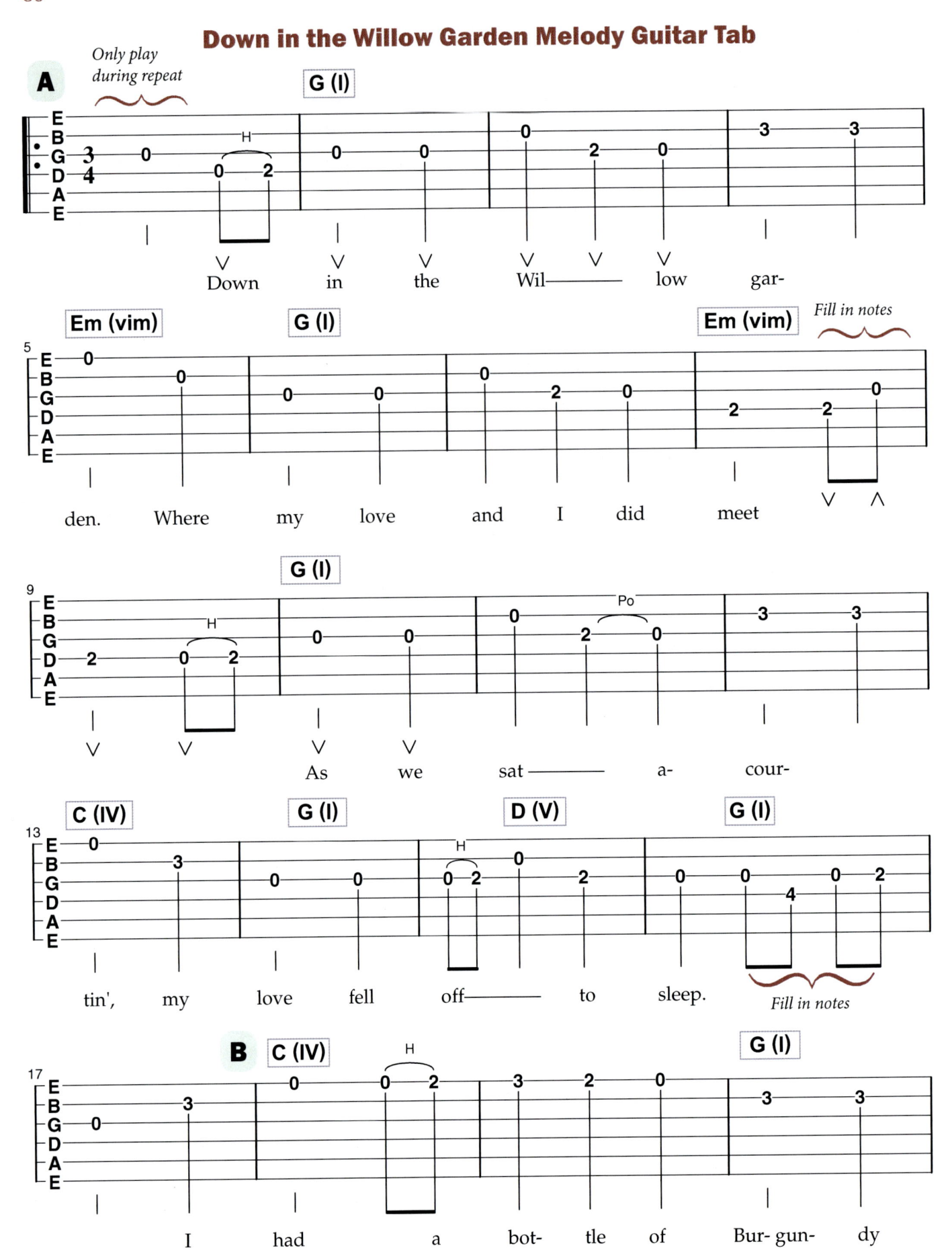

wine. My true love, she did not know.

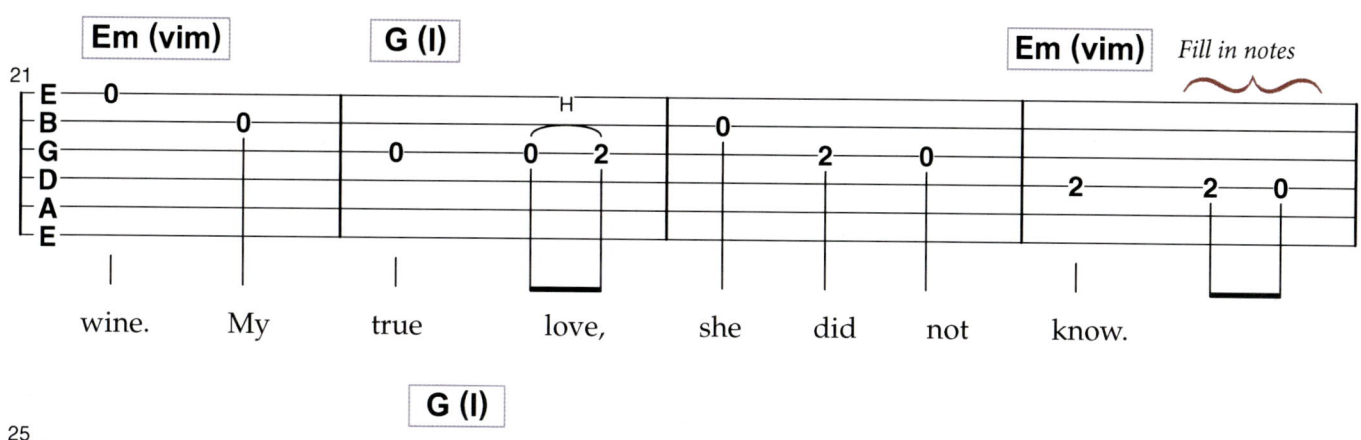

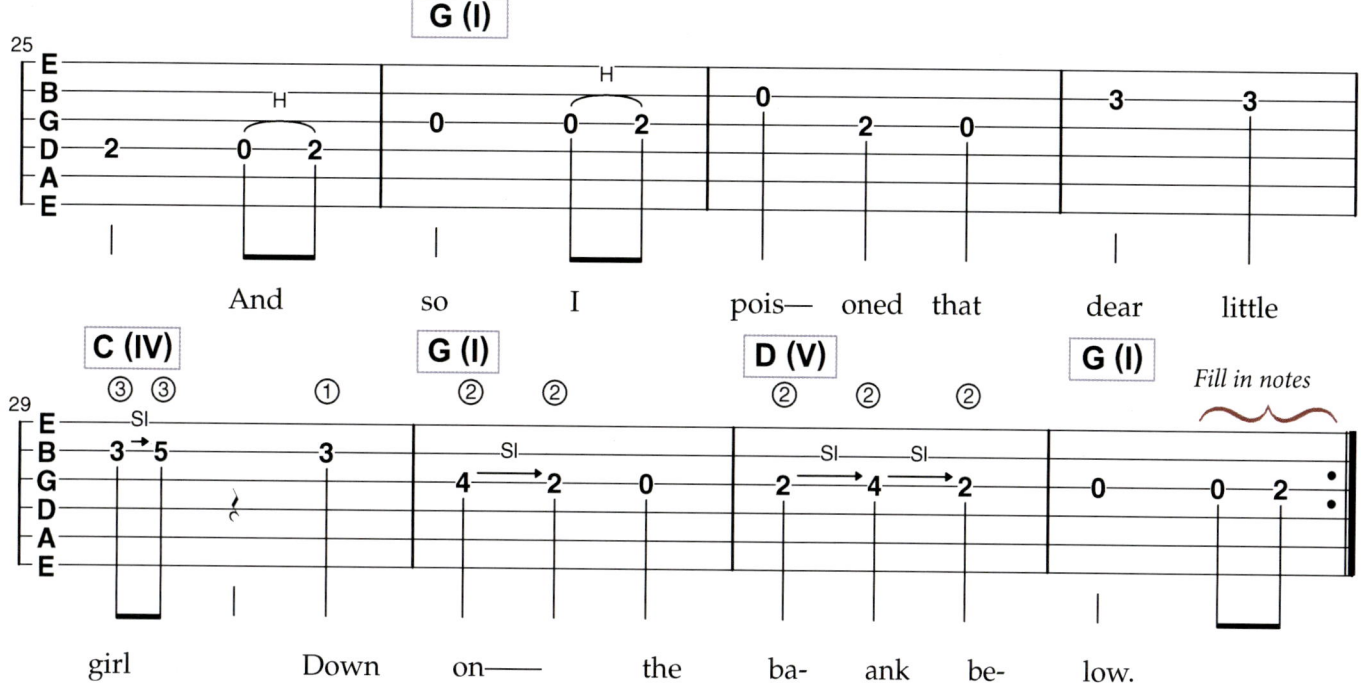

And so I pois— oned that dear little girl Down on the ba- ank be- low.

Verse 2

A

G (I)   Em (vi)
I drew a saber through her

G (I)   Em (vi)
It was a bloody knife

G (I)   C (IV)
I threw her in the river

         G (I)   D (V)   G (I)
Which was a dreadful sign.

B

C (IV)   G (I) Em (vi)
My father often told me

G (I)   Em (vi)
That money would set me free

G (I)   C (IV)
If I would murder that dear little girl

        G (I)   D (V)   G (I)
Whose name was Rose Connolly

Verse 3

A

My father sits at his cabin door
Wiping his tear-dimmed eyes
For his only son soon shall walk
To yonder scaffold high.

B

My race is run, beneath the sun
The scaffold now waits for me
For I did murder that dear little girl
Whose name was Rose Connolly.

Playing Minor Chords

Minor keys and minor chords sound "sad" to most people. They use a flatted 3rd tone, which is a half step lower than the 3rd in a major chord or scale. The next song, Shady Grove, is an old-time, minor key version of the song. For this song, you will use E minor (Em) and D major (D).

You probably remember that to play a major scale, you start with the root tone followed by tones in these intervals (or spacings):

| WHOLE STEP | WHOLE STEP | HALF STEP | WHOLE STEP | WHOLE STEP | WHOLE STEP | HALF STEP |

Which for the key of G major is this:

1	2	3	4	5	6	7	1 (8)
G	A	B	C	D	E	F#	G

Relative Minor Scale

The *relative minor scale* for a key starts with the 6th tone of the major key and walks up the scale notes from there. E minor is the relative minor for the key of G. The Em scale notes are E, F#, G, A, B, C, D (starting on the 6th note in the key of G and walking up the G scale). Notice that this changes our pattern of half and whole steps because we are staring from the 6th tone in the scale but keeping the spacings from the G major scale. This change in the usual interval gives the minor scale its haunting sound.

| WHOLE STEP | HALF STEP | WHOLE STEP | WHOLE STEP | HALF STEP | WHOLE STEP | WHOLE STEP |

| E | F# | G | A | B | C | D | E |

Do you need to memorize this to play Shady Grove? Probably not, but song melodies use mostly the notes in the scale. Knowing how scales work is a good starting point for being able to play any melody you hear.

Minor Chord Recipe

The recipe for a *minor chord* is: 1 + ♭3 + 5. In other words, the root tone (1), the tone one and a half steps up (the flatted 3rd note), and the 5th note of the related scale. Now that you know the "secret recipe" you can figure out other minor chords. Knowledge is power and that can't hurt in guitar playing!

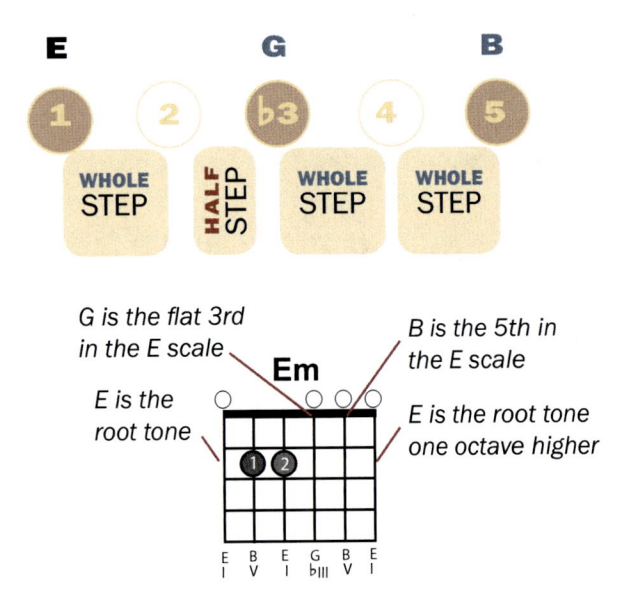

E   G   B

1   2   ♭3   4   5

WHOLE STEP | HALF STEP | WHOLE STEP | WHOLE STEP

G is the flat 3rd in the E scale

E is the root tone

B is the 5th in the E scale

E is the root tone one octave higher

Em

E Minor Scale

The *E minor scale* walks up the G scale starting from E. Of course you can go back down too!

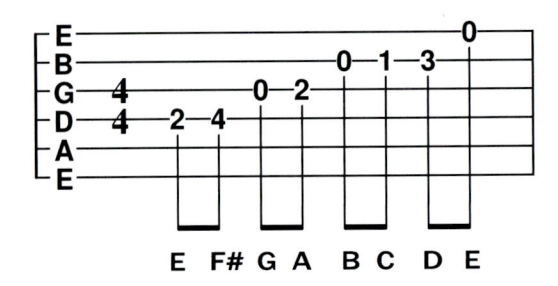

```
E-------------------------0-
B----------------0-1-3------
G------4-------0-2----------
D----4---2-4----------------
A--------------------------
E--------------------------
```

E F# G A B C D E

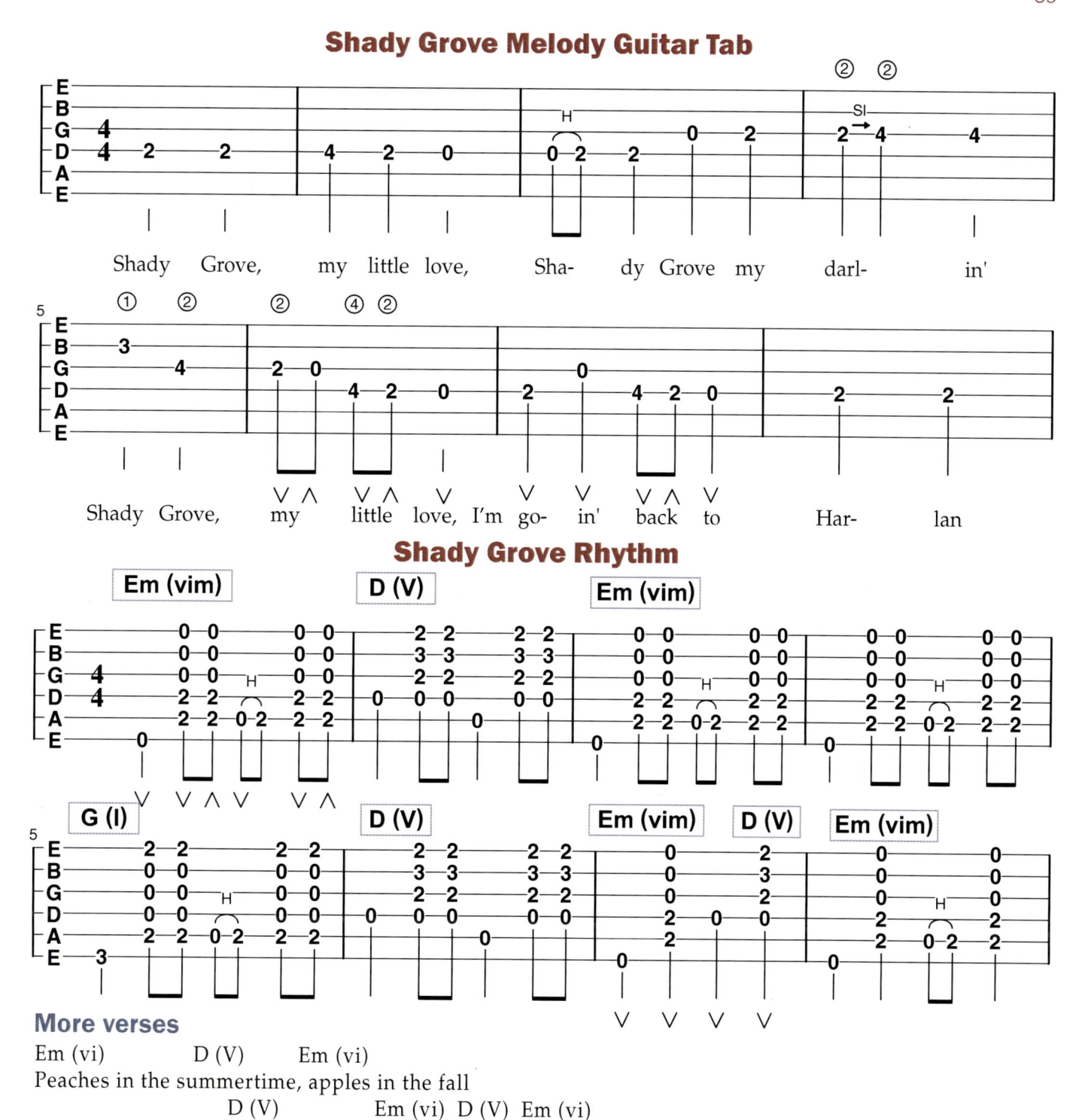

Shady Grove Melody Guitar Tab

[Guitar tablature with lyrics:]
Shady Grove, my little love, Shady Grove my darlin'
Shady Grove, my little love, I'm goin' back to Harlan

Shady Grove Rhythm

[Guitar tablature showing chord progression: Em (vim) — D (V) — Em (vim) — G (I) — D (V) — Em (vim) — D (V) — Em (vim)]

More verses

Em (vi)　　　D (V)　　Em (vi)
Peaches in the summertime, apples in the fall
　　　　　　D (V)　　　　Em (vi) D (V) Em (vi)
If I can't have my Shady Grove, I'll have no one at all

Cheeks as red as a blooming rose, eyes of the deepest brown
She is the darling of my heart, prettiest girl in town

The first time I saw Shady Grove, she was standing at the door
Shoes and stockings in her hand, little bare feet on the floor

Wish I had a guitar string, made of golden twine
Every tune I'd play on it, I wish that girl were mine

Wish I had a needle and thread, fine as I could sew
I'd sew that pretty girl to my side, and down the road I'd go

Some come here to fiddle and dance, some come here to tarry
Some come here to fiddle and dance, I come here to marry

This is the old-time version of Shady Grove. The modern bluegrass version uses the same words, but a different major key melody and chord progression.

Chords for the Key of D

Practice the chords most commonly used when playing in the key of D. D is the I chord, G is the IV, and A the V chord in this key.

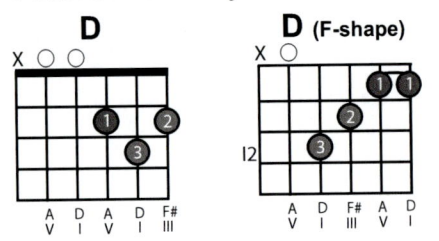

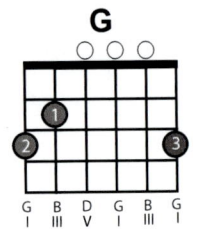

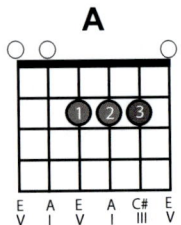

D Scale (Open and Closed)

Practice the D scale with this upper extension used in Angeline the Baker. Two versions of the scale are shown— one where you play the "open" D note on string 4, the other where you play the "closed" D note at fret 5 on string 5. It is the same note, but using the fingered note gives you a movable scale (where you can shift the entire pattern up 2 frets to play in E for example.)

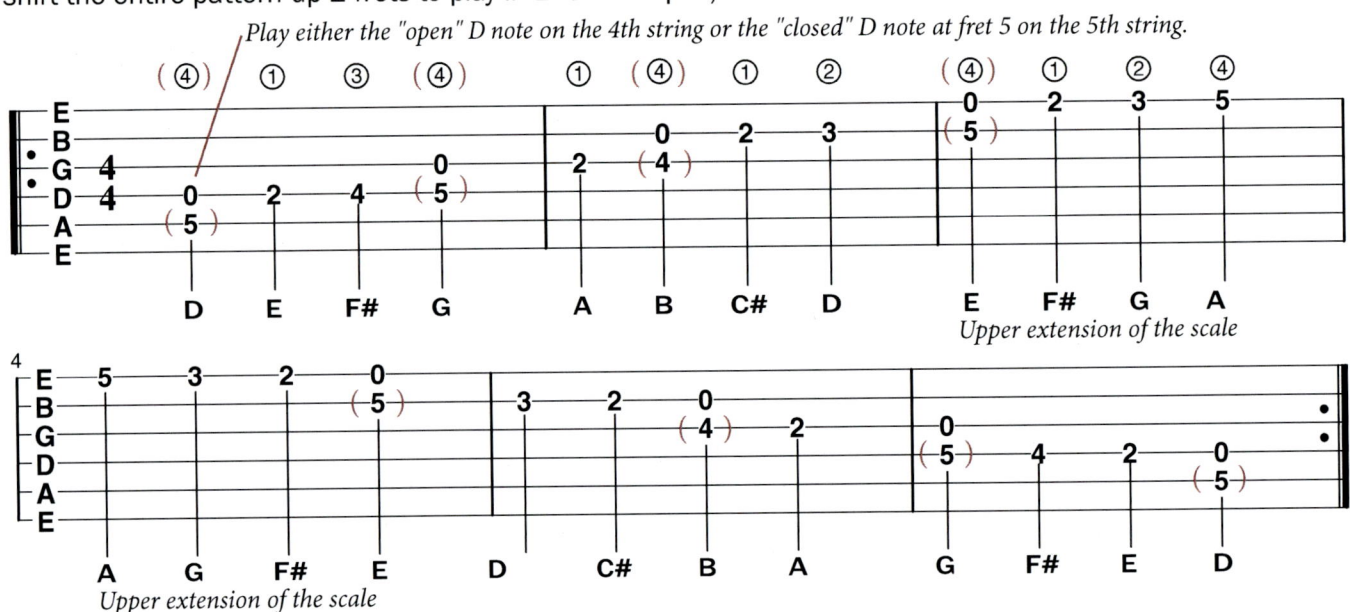

Play either the "open" D note on the 4th string or the "closed" D note at fret 5 on the 5th string.

Movable Two Octave D Scale

This two octave D scale uses closed notes further up the neck for another scale that is easy to move for playing in a different key. Once you master the pattern, try moving every note two frets up the neck to play an E scale. Move each note back two frets to play a C scale.

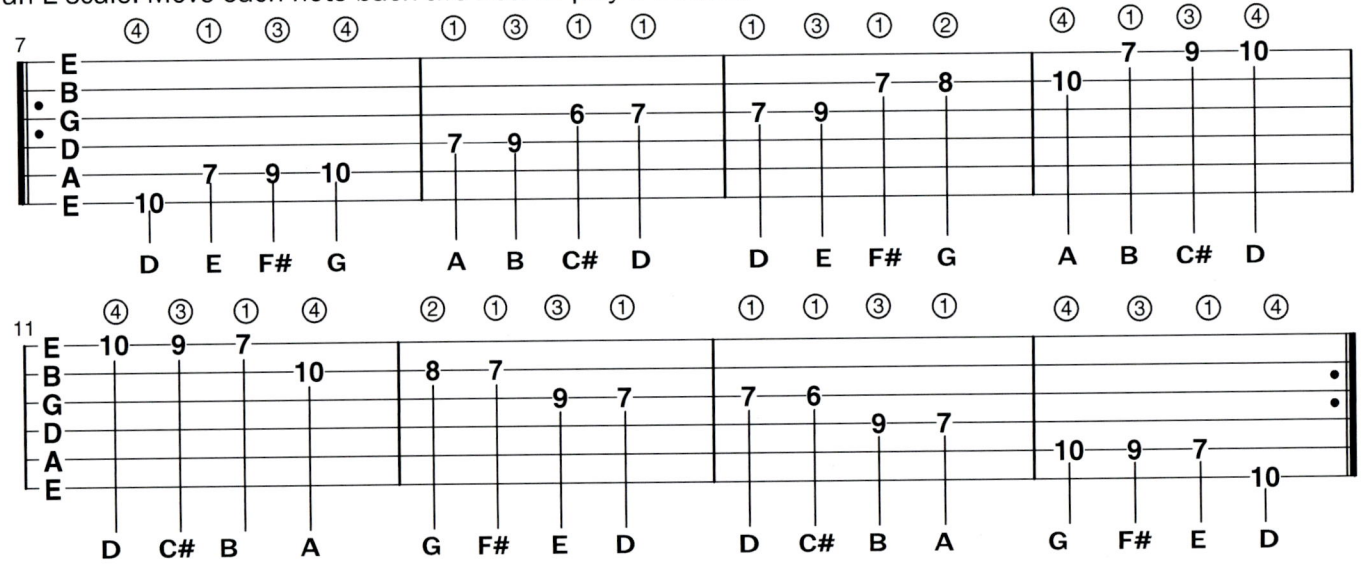

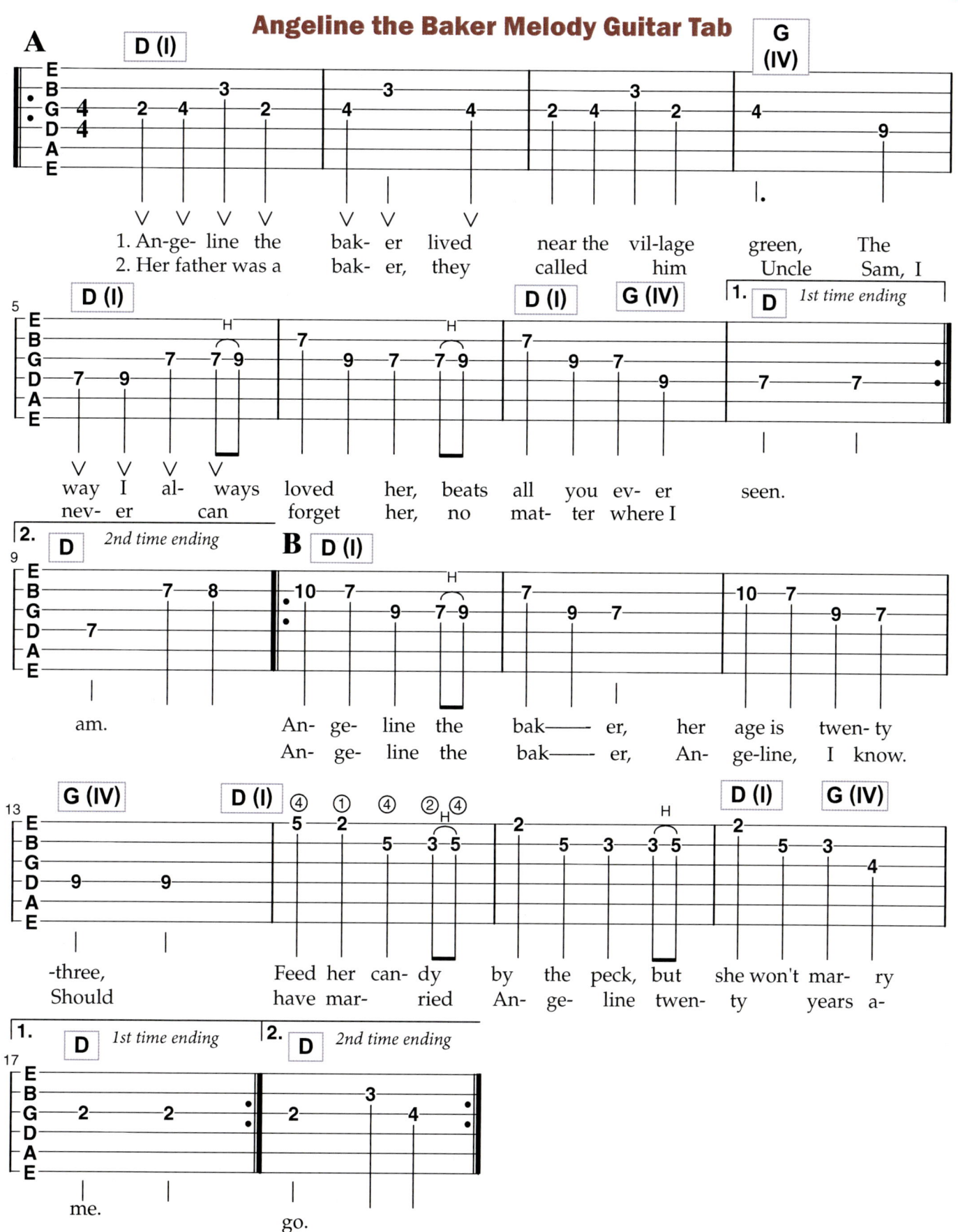

Angeline the Baker Melody Guitar Tab

1. An-ge-line the bak-er lived near the vil-lage green, The
2. Her father was a bak-er, they called him Uncle Sam, I

way I al-ways loved her, beats all you ev-er seen.
nev-er can forget her, no mat-ter where I

am.

An-ge-line the bak—er, her age is twen-ty
An-ge-line the bak—er, An-ge-line, I know.

-three, Feed her can-dy by the peck, but she won't mar-ry
Should have mar-ried An-ge-line twen-ty years a-

me.
go.

Tell how I took Angeline down to the county fair,
Her father chased me halfway home and told me to stay there.

Angeline the Baker, she lived on the village green;
And the way that I love her, beats all to be seen.

She won't do the baking because she is too stout,
She makes cookies by the peck, throws the coffee out.

Angeline the Baker, her age is twenty-three,
Little children round her feet and a guitar on her knee

Guitar Picking Practice

Notice that when picking guitar, you usually alternate down picking then up. Or down strumming then up strumming. Practicing the down/up picking and strumming is the starting point for fast, smooth playing and good rhythmic time. But many other picking and strumming patterns are used in music. Add these and other patterns as part of your practice routine.

Picking Exercise #1

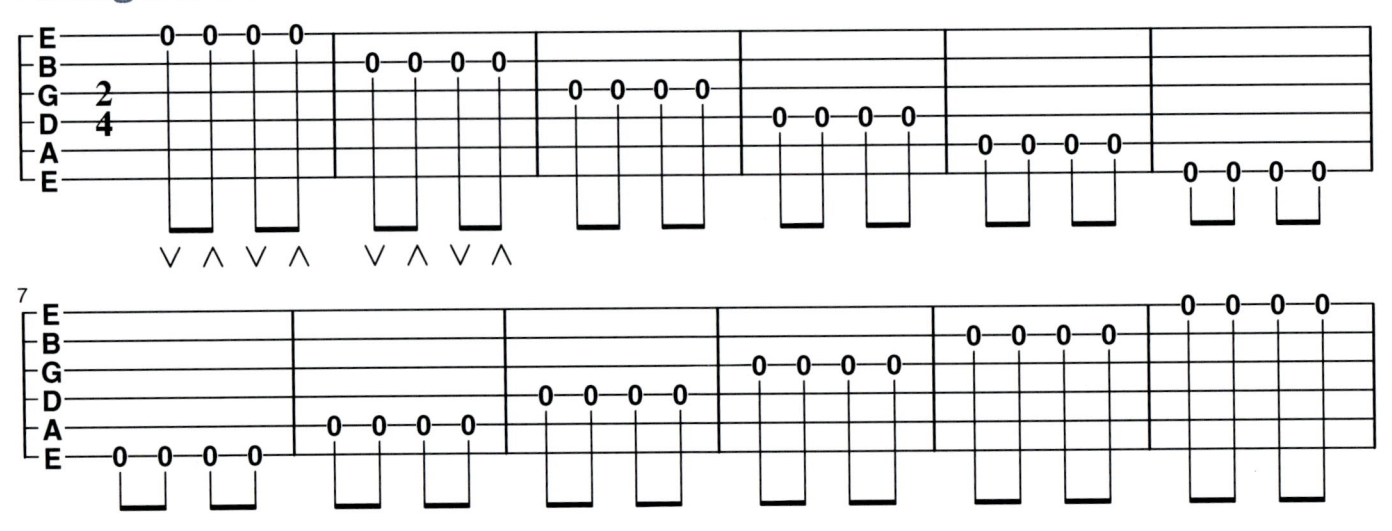

Picking Exercise #2

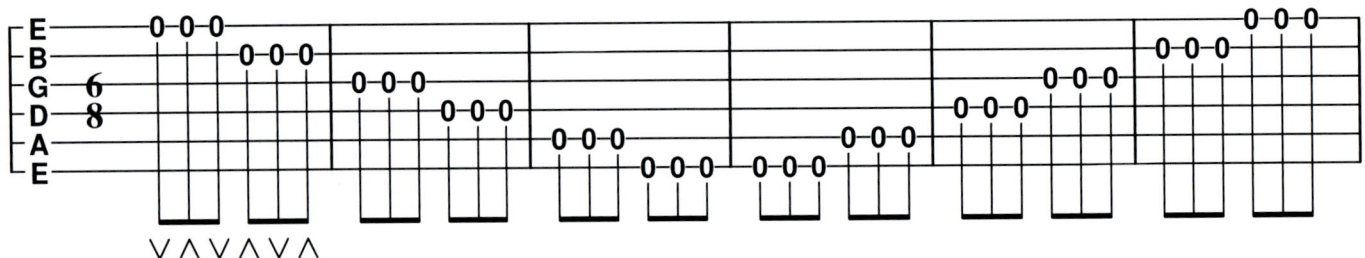

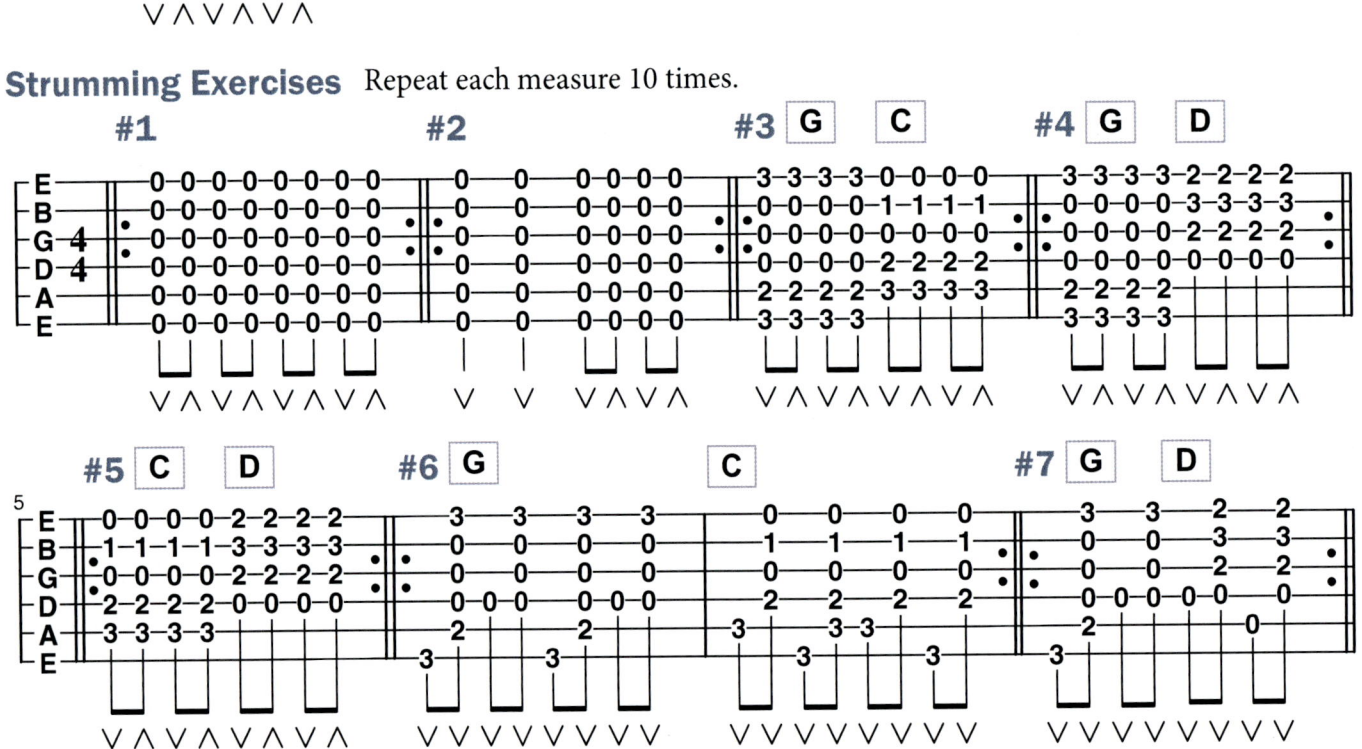

Strumming Exercises Repeat each measure 10 times.

Basic Guitar Chords

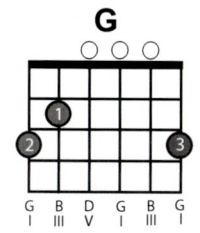

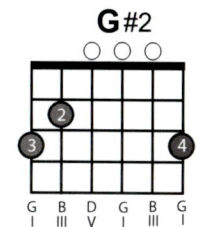

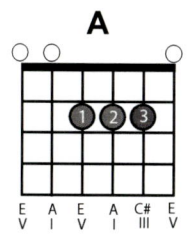

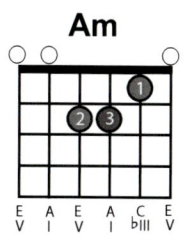

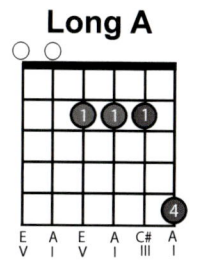

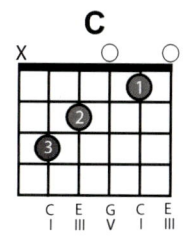

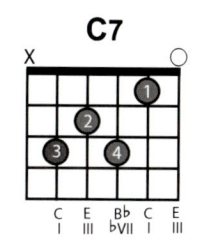

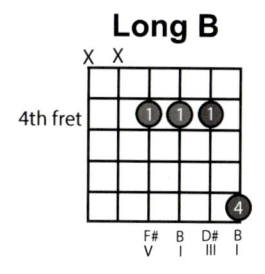

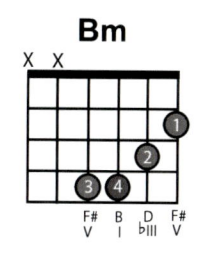

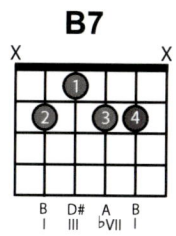

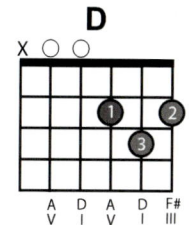

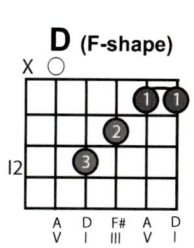

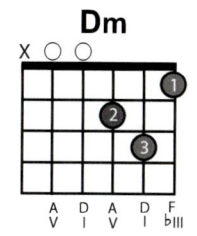

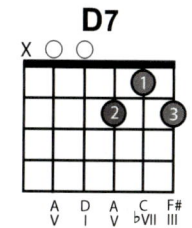

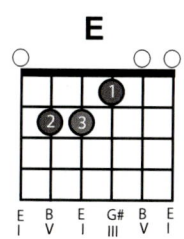

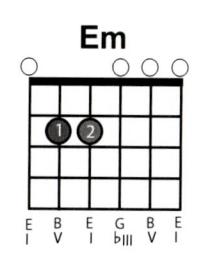

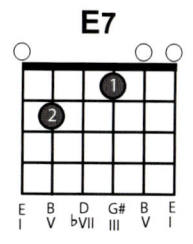

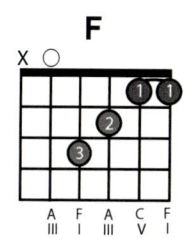

Getting Started with Guitar Chord Shapes

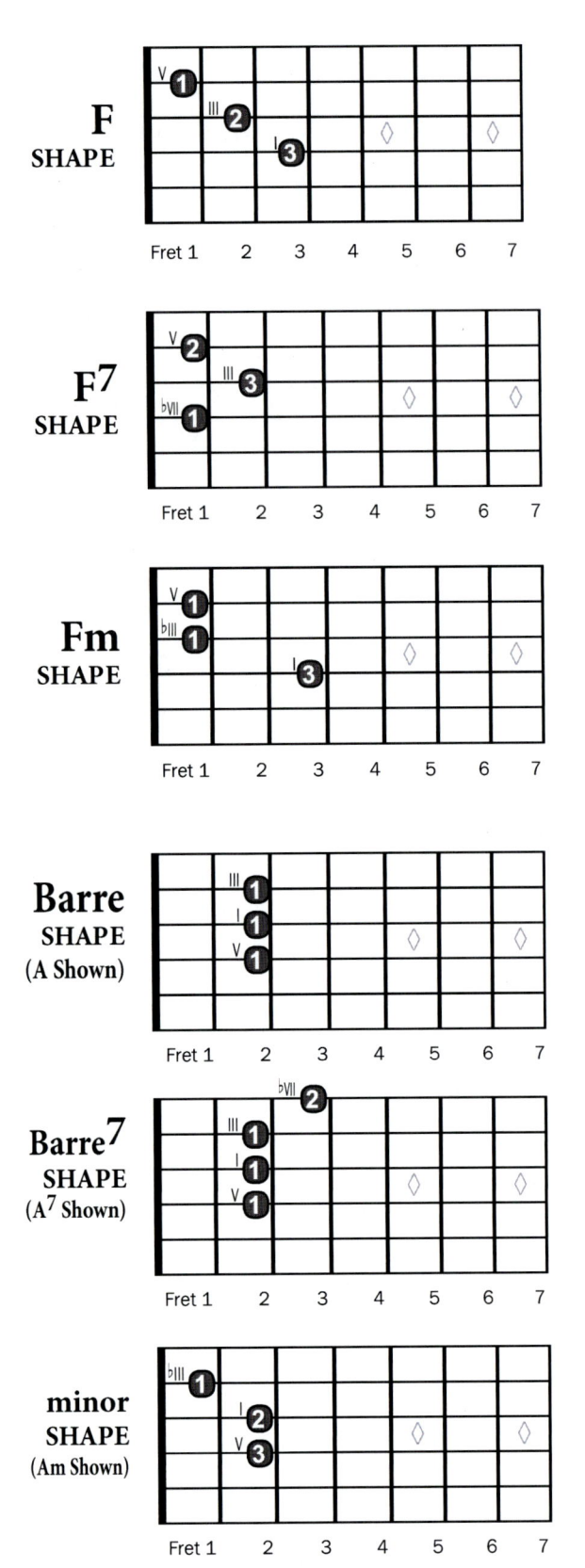

CHORD RECIPES

NAME	SCALE TONES in CHORD			
major	I	III	V	
minor	I	bIII	V	
dom 7th	I	III	V	bVII
minor 7th	I	bIII	V	bVII
maj 7th	I	III	V	VII
6th	I	III	V	VI
aug (+)	I	III	#V	
dim (o)	I	bIII	bV	

F SHAPE

F7 SHAPE

Fm SHAPE

Barre SHAPE (A Shown)

Barre7 SHAPE (A7 Shown)

minor SHAPE (Am Shown)

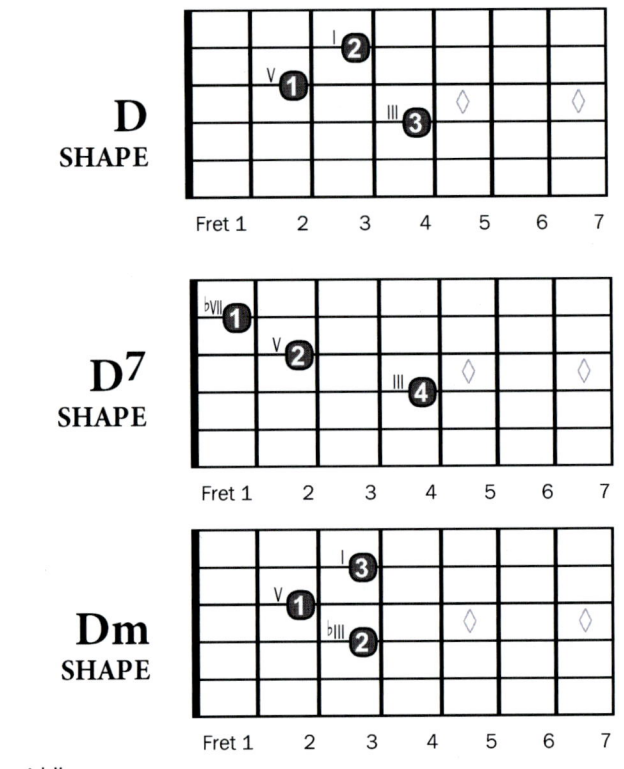

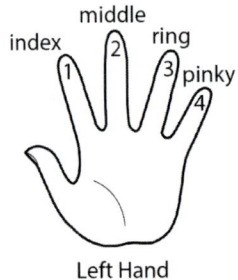

D SHAPE

D7 SHAPE

Dm SHAPE

Left Hand: index 1, middle 2, ring 3, pinky 4

These barre, D, and F chord shapes are an easy way to get started with movable chord shapes. For example, move the barre7 shape from fret 2 (A7) to fret 4 to play B7 (fret 3 to play Bb7), etc. Only strum the strings on which you are playing fretted notes. For example, if you play the minor shape barre (Am) shown, move it up two frets to play Bm, but do not strum string 1.

If you play attention to the open string tones, you can strum them when they are tones in the chord you are playing for example, strum the A string when you play an A chord, but not if you move the shape up two frets to play B.

The chords are not all pictured here, but you can easily figure out where to move them based on your understanding of the scale.

Closed Chord Groups

Work on playing movable chord shapes in groups near each other on the guitar neck. For more advanced playing, you will want to quickly change chords and finding one close by on the neck will help. Also practice walking the same chord shape up and down the neck, saying the chord names as you go.

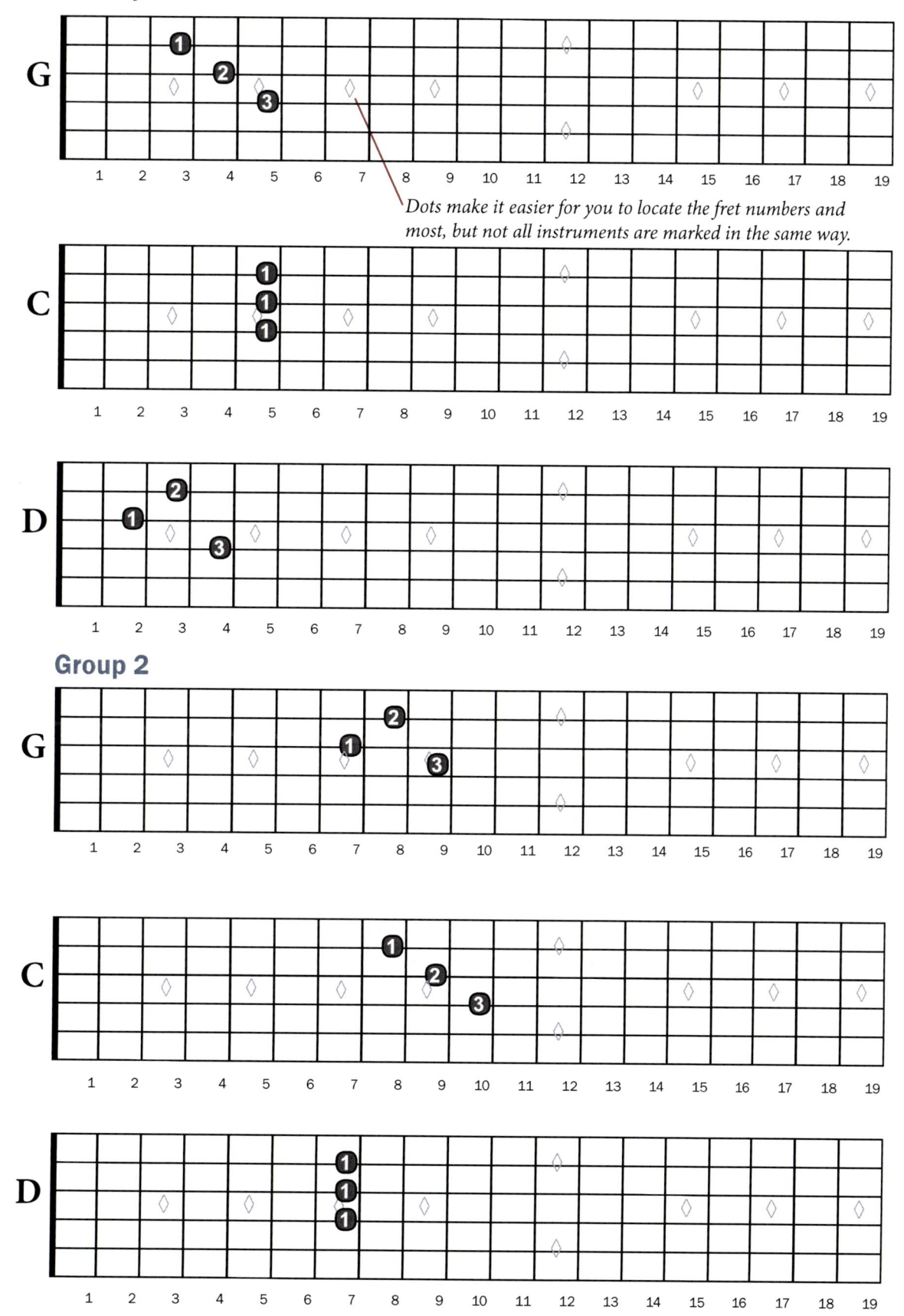

Group 1

Dots make it easier for you to locate the fret numbers and most, but not all instruments are marked in the same way.

Group 2

Group 3

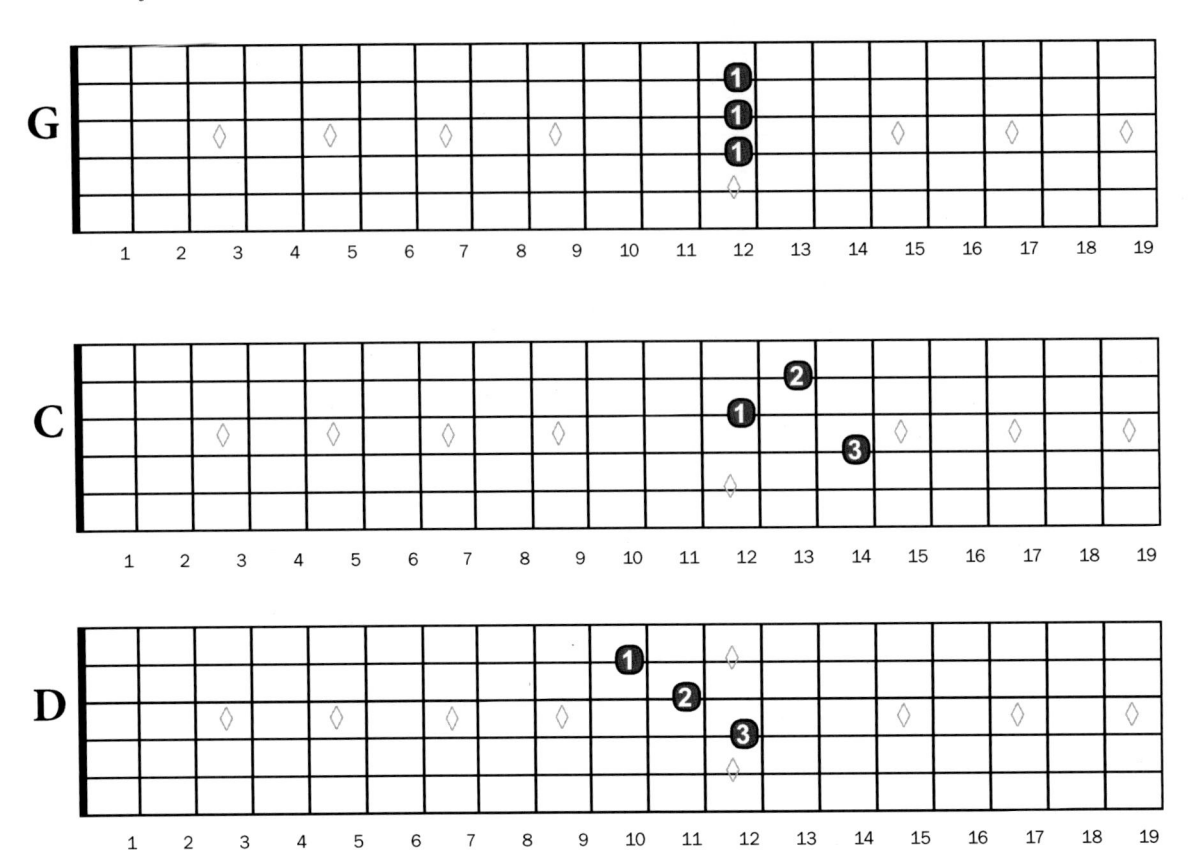

G

C

D

Made in the USA
Middletown, DE
02 April 2024

52463046R00029